CAT COUNTRY

CAT COUNTRY

The Quest for the British Big Cat

DI FRANCIS

DAVID & CHARLES
Newton Abbot   London   North Pomfret (Vt)

Dedicated to the hundreds of people who have come forward with sightings and without whom this book would never have been written, but especially to John Bastin for his help, Malcolm Price for his companionship, Ann Maggs for her friendship, and to everyone who has had close encounters of the cat kind. Thank you.

British Library Cataloguing in Publication Data

Francis, Di
    Cat country.
    1. Pumas
    I. Title
    636.8'9   QL737.C2
    ISBN 0–7153–8425–2

Text © Di Francis 1983

Photoset in Plantin by
Northern Phototypesetting Co, Bolton
and printed in Great Britain by
A. Wheaton & Co, Hennock Road, Exeter
for David & Charles (Publishers) Limited
Brunel House Newton Abbot Devon

Published in the United States of America
by David & Charles Inc
North Pomfret Vermont 05053 USA

Contents

And no one has a right to say that no water-babies exist, till they have seen no water-babies existing; which is quite a different thing, mind, from not seeing water-babies.

Charles Kingsley, *The Water Babies*

Introduction

While collecting the interviews for this book I found myself, a journalist, on the other side, being interviewed by press and other media. One of the most frequently asked questions was 'Why?' Why was I interested in the possibility that large cats are living wild in the British Isles? Why was I so determined to find out what they were? Why was I writing a book about them? Why was I willing to spend a great deal of my time living in uncomfortable and sometimes dangerous conditions just to prove they were there?

Sometimes I asked myself the same questions. And I could never really answer any of them to my own satisfaction. For the media I resorted to the old chestnut 'Because they're there!' But my reasons were far more complex. In the beginning I also had to search deeply into my conscience as to whether it was in the best interest of the animals themselves to be 'discovered'. Would the public accept calmly the knowledge that it wasn't just fairies that might be at the bottom of their gardens, or would they rush American-style to the nearest gunsmith, arming themselves against this dangerous wild animal? The answer to this problem must be information: and people must be reminded that the animals have lived at the bottom of their gardens for hundreds of years without ever doing worse than an occasional raid on the hen-run or the dustbin. This can be done gently, so that we accept the presence of the cats at the bottom of other people's gardens before being faced with one at the bottom of our own.

Farmers are a different problem. Most cats hunt across farmland and however much I wish to proclaim their blameless lives, they do now and then account for livestock, whether the occasional duck or hen or a raid into the grazing sheep or goats.

Luckily most farmers are – in their own way – conservationists. Not in the matter of hedgerows perhaps, but a man who lives on the land can't detach himself from nature. However mechanised the process of farming becomes, the farmer is still a man who can listen to the early morning song of the thrush, who can take pleasure in the scent of damp clover and new-mown hay. So the art will be to persuade the hard-working farmer that the animal kills enough rabbits and vermin to make it useful on the land and that therefore its occasional lapses are forgivable.

But should the animal be officially discovered? Would it not be better to let it exist as it has done for hundreds, perhaps thousands, of years, quietly getting on with the business of surviving, ignoring the existence of man and in return being ignored? Undoubtedly yes, if life could happily continue as it has done. Its peaceful existence, however, is threatened.

As farming methods change, so do the fields. No longer is this green and pleasant land the patchwork of little fields, divided by small copses and fringed with woodland, that our ancestors knew. As the mighty mechanical monsters take over, so the fields become vast expanses of carefully ordered crops. Gone are the hedgerows and tree clumps where the Saxons planted their hazels and elders. And as the price of land rises, farmers are forced to look again at the non-productive stretches of scrub and woodland. When the diggers move in, the wildlife moves out. If the felling and clearing continue over the next twenty years, the cat's chance to continue its lifestyle is virtually nil. Only a few pockets of remote and inaccessible forest will remain and the cat will face a choice of changing its habitat or dying out. And the only change it can make will bring it to the notice of the public – a public unprepared for the sight of leopard-sized cats inhabiting the British countryside. So its best chance seems to be discovery, classification and then protection as an endangered species. At the time of writing, as the animal does not officially exist, any person seeing one can blast it to eternity with a shotgun. If it isn't really there, then it doesn't matter if it's killed. At least, that appears to be the rather tangled working of our protection of wild animals laws. After all, you can only protect what you know exists. Yet if I declared I was off to blow up the Loch Ness monster, I'm sure that a public outcry would result, despite the fact that, according to the desk-bound scientists, the creature has no more existence than these cats.

Perhaps the greatest enemies of these splendid creatures are, unwittingly, the well-meaning people who believe in them for the wrong reasons. Too many people are ready to gasp 'supernatural' at anything natural that they themselves don't understand. This is typically illustrated in the case of the so-called water monsters, such as the Loch Ness sightings. Whether there is a living creature there or not I'm not qualified to say; but I do feel qualified to comment on claims made in books or the press by people who wish to show that the creatures are of another world. One of the favourite ideas is that the creatures must be supernatural because cameras refuse to operate correctly when they appear. Well, a large number of photographs have been taken at Loch Ness and other stretches of water, and however inconclusive these are, the fact remains that the cameras did their job. Cameras do jam – if I was suddenly faced with a living legend, whether expected or otherwise, I've no doubt that in the excitement of the moment I might be attacked by a well-known human phenomenon, becoming 'all fingers and thumbs'; in the panic of the moment I would probably press the wrong button, get my focus wrong or even forget to remove the lens cover. And even the scientists are human.

Photographic evidence is one of the great criteria of the boffins. If it was there, someone would have photographed it. Well yes, if the entire population of this country went around with cameras draped round their necks twenty-four hours a day. Or if the obliging creature, on being spotted, would calmly wait, giving the witness time to rush home to get his camera or even grab it from the back of the car. Unfortunately, these essentially elusive unknown creatures are never that helpful in assisting their own discovery. On being spotted, their main thought is to put as much distance as possible between themselves and the witness as fast as possible. And often this feeling is shared by the panic-stricken witness.

And even photographs won't alter the opinions of the true sceptic. After all, there have been a large number of pictures taken of what may be the elusive Loch Ness monster, yet the general opinion is still that the creature lives not in the peaty waters of the loch but rather in the amber waters of the Scottish whisky. And a classic recent case concerns another creature of legend and mystic, the American Big Foot. Throughout the United States and parts of Canada for the last hundred years, people have been reporting sightings of a large hairy manlike creature very similar to the Yeti or Abominable Snowman of the Himalayas. Before the arrival of the white man, the Red Indians had a number of legends about the creature. On 20 October 1967, Roger Patterson and Bob Gimlin were near Bluff Creek in northern California when they spotted a large manlike hairy creature. They took a ciné-film of the creature before it retreated into the forest. But was it conclusive proof ?' 'A man dressed in a hairy skin,' was the cry. 'It can't be an ape because it doesn't walk like one,' was another. Walk like what? Yet the film has been extensively examined and the estimated height of the creature is believed to be 6ft 8in and its weight approximately 440lb. Despite this film, the numerous reports of sightings and the hundreds of casts taken of strange manlike footprints, people still shake their heads and mutter that it is impossible that a large manlike animal could exist officially undiscovered today.

And if unknown creatures living in the vastness of the American wilderness are incredible, how much harder it is to accept the existence of a large carnivore in this tiny overcrowded island of ours. Yet the evidence is there – the eyewitnesses, the casts of footprints. But still the boffins sit comfortably behind their desks and shake their heads sadly: 'How marvellous, if only it was true.' But it is true and that is why I am writing this book: to try and prove it.

Three questions are usually asked by reporters, interviewers and the man in the street: 'Are they really there? What are they?

How many are there?' At the time of writing, I can only answer the first question with any certainty. Yes, they are there, and hopefully this book will show it. Answers to the other two are much more difficult. The answer to what they are must finally depend on the capture and full study of one of the animals, which is now my aim. Until someone succeeds, we can only examine the evidence we have and hypothesise. The moment a living specimen is trapped the question will be answered. It might be tomorrow, it might take a year or ten; but it will happen.

As to the question of how many there are, we may never exactly know. At present I can only give an indication by showing the whereabouts of territories, estimating the number of animals seen and suggesting other areas suitable for them. It will take many years of research before we can have a fairly accurate idea of the numbers involved throughout the whole of the British Isles. At least the populated areas are easier than the remote parts.

Once a study centre is set up, people will be able to lift a phone to report sightings. These can then be charted. Areas producing a large number of reports can be fully investigated and the approximate number of animals to an area can be estimated. For example, let us take an imaginary forested area in Berkshire called Woodland. Over a twelve-month period twenty people phone the centre with sightings. When these reports are compared they are divided into groups. Ten witnesses have reported seeing black cats, five have seen reddish-brown animals and five describe the animals as spotted or striped. These sightings would suggest that Woodland contains a breeding group of at least three identifiable animals. A careful comparison of the reports breaks the group down even further. Detailed descriptions produce a black cat almost as big as a Great Dane dog, a black cat the size of a spaniel, a dark reddish-brown cat the size of a Great Dane, a golden-tawny lion-like cat and finally a brown cat the size of a Labrador dog with a striped and spotted coat. Our breeding group appears to have grown from three to at least five separate animals. At this stage an investigating team would move into the area, combing the woods. Casts of pugmarks would be taken and compared. This could confirm there were indeed five animals, or else it could bring to light extra cats that had avoided the public's eye, or resembled other animals in size and colour; there could be four adult animals the size of a Great Dane, not three. After a few weeks or even months the team would be pretty certain how many animals lived in the territory of Woodland, their sex and approximate age, whether adults, cubs or juveniles. This whole operation would have to be repeated all over the country to give an estimate of the number of animals. It would be time-consuming and use manpower, but at least would be a fairly straightforward task.

This is not so where the cats have managed to avoid all contact with man in tracts of countryside that are isolated from towns and villages – the big ranges of the Scottish Highlands, the remote Cambrian and Black Mountains of Wales, the Cumbrian Mountains of the Lake District, for instance. Where do we start looking? The first step is to know the cats, understand their way of life, their habitat and behaviour; then we can search for areas that would meet their requirements. It is a big task but there is no alternative. It has been done in other countries; a census of the European lynx was conducted in this way, and a survey was made to estimate the number of remaining wild tigers. At least we don't have to contend with the vast land tracts involved in those searches. We might have some reasonably difficult terrain to cope with, but we don't have inaccessible and dangerous rain forests or tropical jungles; nor do we have to contend with other dangerous wild animals. In comparison with other countries, we are a tamed and tiny island, and our regions of wilderness have shrunk down to reasonable size. So the search is not impossible.

All this is looking far into the future. The first task is to show that the animal exists; the second is to convince people that it needs protection. The rest should follow. Once the experts have to accept that the creature really is around our countryside, then they will come out of hibernation, shake the museum dust from themselves and tackle the task of identifying it with enthusiasm. Whatever the cat is, it is certainly endangered; therefore funds should be forthcoming from august bodies like the World Wildlife Fund to back a survey and protection plan. Perhaps an even more important task than convincing the experts is to convince the public that the creature is not dangerous. It is not sitting in the treetops waiting to pounce on unwary walkers or lurking to rob cribs of innocent babes. It is a shy creature with little interest in the behaviour of man. However, it is large enough to do considerable damage if provoked or cornered, so like all large wild animals it needs to be treated with respect. There are times when non-aggressive animals can become dangerous: when frightened, when hungry and when defending their young. For a year I have spent a great deal of my time in the forest areas tracking the cats, both day and night, and my own behaviour shows that I have learned that it is not dangerous. I have never carried anything more defensive than a camera (and I have no form of death wish or posthumous-fame ambitions). But I have always followed certain rules. When tracking a mother with a cub, I've avoided entering, alone, any place that I consider could be the den area. I have seldom entered an enclosed space where the animal might be. I have always given it an escape route to use if we meet. I've treated the cat with respect and I've never been afraid of it. I've perhaps felt unease when approaching den areas, but no more than I would feel approaching a swarm of bees.

However, the general public have not always obeyed such rules. At Tedburn St Mary in Devon, after a number of sightings in the spring of 1981, people made it their Sunday outing to try and spot the so-called puma. The woods were filled with family groups, with young children racing through the bushes. Stupid as this behaviour was, there was worse to come. Children scoured the area on horseback. Imagine the reaction of a normally docile pony on suddenly being confronted with a large leopard-sized cat. Anyone who has spent some time with horses knows that some of them have a tendency to sidestep when on roads, directly into the path of oncoming traffic. This behaviour is not perverseness but is directly linked through race memory with a fear of treading too close to bushes or clumps of trees that might be hiding a predator. Although our modern horses have never had to contend with a lion lying in wait in the local brambles, their instinct isn't going to let them take any chances. And therefore, on meeting a large cat-like carnivore, their instinct will undoubtedly tell them that they are faced with danger and must get away from it as quickly as possible. Not many little girl Sunday riders could cope with a bolting pony, especially in woodland. I believe that the inoffensiveness of the creature is proved by the fact that no one has been harmed – not even foolish people that take noisy dogs and young children into its territory when it has young. For the Tedburn St Mary cat appeared just a few days later with a tiny cub trailing behind it.

Another question often asked is 'How long have they been there?' This may be answered at the same time as we discover for certain what they are. For instance, a hybrid could have been around for just a few years, but a 'new' species would in fact be very old, dating from the last great ice age. Some idea can be gauged by research into legends and old newspaper files. It can't be conclusive proof but it is useful to know that in 1860 a man claimed he met a lion walking along a woodland path. The man might have been a liar, mistaken or drunk, or he might indeed have met a lion that had just escaped from a local travelling fair. However, if a dozen men over twenty years have claimed that they have met lions in the same area, then it becomes a stronger possibility that the woodland was indeed the home of a large lion-like cat. If the reports stretch over fifty years, then the possibility has to be faced that the one animal has become a breeding group because the sightings have covered at least two life-spans of a big cat. It is in this way that the evidence has to be collected and examined to try and ascertain how long the animals have been living in an area and whether they appear to have been breeding. Unfortunately, even now people do not report their sightings for fear of being laughed at. It must have taken a lot of courage in the superstitious past to stand up and swear you'd seen an animal that you hadn't even seen in a picture. Today most people would

Introduction

have some idea of the appearance of a puma or a lion, but in the past few would have known what they looked like.

It was because of this that I began to examine the Black Dog legends closely. Modern cat sightings produce details of coat, size, attitude and tail, but the head shape and ears are often omitted. In the panic of the moment the witnesses take in the overall appearance of the creature but miss the smaller details. How difficult it must have been to see details by the light of a swinging lantern if they can be missed in the full beam of a car's headlights or a torch. I had always wondered how people distinguished ghost or devil 'Black Dogs' from the genuine article just going for a nightly walk. After all, if I spotted a black dog padding up the lane behind me, I wouldn't give it a second look. What was it about the so-called Black Dogs that sent practical farm workers and hard-headed merchants screaming in terror to the nearest church for protection? Was it possible that the dogs were not dogs at all, but large black cats? To be confronted in a dark lane by a snarling leopard-like animal would certainly induce fear in all but the very stout-hearted. And if the witnesses were asked afterwards what they had seen, who could blame them if they likened the creature to the nearest animal they understood of similar build and shape?

The Black Dog legends appear all over the British Isles and are of two basic types: the Devil Hound and the Companion Dog. I first eliminated all the stories of companion-type dogs from my research. These concern the devoted fox terrier that is still seen at its master's fireside many years after its death, or the animal that appears to a specific family over the years to forewarn them of a change of fortune or a death. I carefully sifted through the rest, removing any that closely identified a specific breed of dog. For instance, no one could mistake a Jack Russell for a cat. The remaining legends were largely about large black smooth-coated dogs with eyes that blazed like red coals and a snarl that resembled a jeering grin. Some dogs appeared to be silent, vanishing into the darkness within seconds of being spotted, but others were audible, like the Shriker or Trash of Lancashire, so called because of the strange sound its feet made and its unearthly screaming. The Hell Dog of Laugharne in Wales also screamed, but the one at Haverfordwest roared. Certainly the Devil Hounds sounded more like cats than any dogs I know.

Once again one is faced with the intellectuals delving into the legends to add to and enhance the mystery. Apparently Ethel H. Rudkin felt that 'the Black Dog has to do with an invasion by water, up the main rivers then up the tributary streams to the springline'. Ivan Bunn, whilst researching into the East Anglian Black Dog, also noted the proximity of water. Janet and Colin Bord suggested the streams might follow ley lines and Steve Moore went further: he produced a theory involving the universal balancing principles of Yin and Yang! No one appears to have thought of the possibility of flesh-and-blood animals needing to drink. After all, it has long been known that the best place to view wild animals is at a waterhole. At least one student of Trinity College in Dublin was ready to admit that he could not decide if what he saw was a dog or a panther!

If enough circumstantial evidence exists to link the Black Dogs of the past with the black cats people see now and then today, then it opens the gates for other exciting possibilities. Firstly it suggests that the cats have been around for hundreds of years, and commonsense increases the hundreds to thousands. Secondly it could explain old mysteries that have been considered unsolvable. Take the Devil's Hoofprints for instance. In 1855, after a heavy fall of snow, the inhabitants of Devon awoke to find that strange hoofprints had crossed over 40 miles of their countryside. The devil had left cloven hoofmarks across fields, over roofs, through gardens and along the tops of high walls. The country was in the grip of superstitious dread. To quote a recent publication *Unexplained*, 'What could have covered large areas of snowbound countryside in a short space of time, undeterred by obstacles, running in a fast mincing step and leaving a hoof-shaped footprint?' What indeed?

Another creature of legend was the Girt Dog of Ennerdale. A huge dog with a yellow coat striped with grey terrorised the district of Ennerdale, killing sheep, in 1810. One witness described the animal as a lion, not a dog. Certainly there are few, if any, breeds of dog that could produce such a colouring. However, records of the legends are fairly well documented, a number of eyewitness statements being preserved, and although it is not possible to prove what the creatures were after so many years, it is possible to examine the evidence and build up a reasonable case.

But the most important evidence lies in the present, not in the past. I have talked to a great number of people who have seen the big cats of Britain. They come from all walks of life – farmers, teachers, scientists, housewives, policemen, doctors and vets. I have also examined police statements and statements made by members of the public to the police. Each of these is prefaced by the following words: 'This statement is true to the best of my knowledge and belief and I make it knowing that, if it is tendered in evidence, I shall be liable to prosecution if I have wilfully stated in it anything which I know to be false or do not believe to be true.' A strong enough warning and surely enough to deter the average joker. Yet hundreds of people have signed such statements in police stations all over the country, each swearing to have had a close encounter with a big cat. A number have been made by the police themselves, for in some cases witnesses have called the police and patrols have arrived before the animal has left the scene. Other policemen have spotted the animals when driving on night patrol. Yet still the boffins shake their heads and suggest that witnesses are either mistaken, drunk or even mad.

Until we have the final proof, a captured animal, we have to collect and examine the evidence available to us. The following chapters attempt to do this monumental task. But this is only the tip of the iceberg. Many hundreds of people have seen a large cat but have been frightened of reporting it for fear of ridicule. Others have been driving home at night and have not dared notify the authorities for fear of being breathalysed. And one man I interviewed actually shot one of the cats eighteen years ago but kept quiet for fear he had broken the law.

Introduction

For those people who have seen the animals, this book is to reassure them that they aren't alone. For they do not need any proof of the animals' existence. For the rest, they must read on and decide for themselves. Are hundreds of respectable people all over the country drunk, mad or liars? Or is there really a large undiscovered carnivore living and breeding throughout the British Isles?

I have divided this book into chapters. The first and of course most important contains modern eyewitness accounts. When possible I have personally checked the statements, either by interviewing the witnesses or by talking to staff at the police stations involved. Others are from letters received personally during the course of my investigations.

Other chapters deal with and compare the known big cats of today, investigate the possibility of an unknown species surviving from the ice age and look at the history of the evolution of the cat. To try and ascertain how long the cats have been around, I have investigated folk-tales, for if indeed the 'Black Dogs' are Black Cats, they have been with us for hundreds of years. And then I rest my case with one last piece of evidence from Wales.

Let the people speak for themselves — those lucky enough to have had close encounters of the cat kind.

1
Eyewitness Accounts

Scotland

Much of Scotland is a beautiful wild country of lonely places, towering mountains, bleak stretches of windswept moorlands and deep untrodden forests. And Scotland is the home of the European wild cat. But it isn't only this known wild cat that haunts its forests: throughout the country, from Glasgow to Tongue in Sutherland, people have been reporting sightings of puma-like or panther-like big cats, far bigger than the native wild cat.

The first recorded evidence of big cats in Scotland can be found in the writings of sixteenth-century chronicler Ralph Holinshed, 'Lions we have had very many in the north parts of Scotland and those with manes of no less force than those of Mauretania; but how and when they were destroyed as yet I do not read.' Just what animals Ralph Holinshed is referring to is unclear. Certainly Britain had lions way back in the ice age, but we would hardly expect Holinshed to know that in the sixteenth century. So is he referring to creatures that have been known in modern times?

The *Daily Express* reported on 14 January 1927 that, following a number of livestock being killed and strange footprints being discovered, a farmer killed 'a large, fierce yellow animal of unknown species'. However, the slaughter continued. Another animal similar to the first was shot, then a third was trapped. 'The body was sent to the London Zoo where it was identified as that of a Lynx.' However, London Zoo has no record in its files of receiving the animal, and one wonders, anyway, just what exactly was sent for identification. The creature was shot in Inverness-shire and without freezing the body would be in a rather advanced state of decomposition on arrival. If it was just the skin that was dispatched to London, a true identification was unlikely. Big cats are being seen today in Inverness-shire, but although they sometimes resemble lynxes, they cannot be identified as that species.

Despite many years of sightings of big cats in the area, it is only recently that police have taken them seriously, and even then, as elsewhere, it is because one man has decided to take a personal interest − in this case Detective Sergeant Cathcart of the Inverness-shire police. Having interviewed witnesses, he felt that the animals were a reality and from 1976 he kept a record of all sightings that came to his notice.

The first of these was a report by an elderly lady, Miss Jessie Chisholm, who lives in an isolated cottage adjacent to the forestry plantation at Cannich in Inverness-shire. One August evening in 1976, she heard a lot of noise coming from her hens and went out to investigate the disturbance. She was amazed to see a beautiful pure black cat, larger than a Labrador dog. She watched it from a distance of about $2\frac{1}{2}$yd as it stared at her for about two minutes. It appeared to be moulting and had a thick tail which was longer than its body.

In January of the following year, when the snow was on the ground, she saw a black cat coming through the trees towards her cottage. It was larger than the animal in the first sighting, but she thought it might be the first one grown up. This cat had some white about the face and a long shiny tail. It leapt over the 6ft high forestry gate and disappeared into the wood.

At about 2.00pm on 27 October 1979, a neighbour of Miss Chisholm, Mr Ted Noble of Kerrow Farm, was on the open hillside collecting his sheep when he spotted an animal which he at first mistook for a hind, near some Shetland ponies. Puzzled by its apparent crouched position he watched it. It got up and ran a few yards towards the ponies and then crouched down again in a typical stalking manner. He realised that the creature was of the cat family and thought it was a lioness because of its size and tawny colour. He immediately reported his sighting to the police. The following day a search of the hillside and surrounding area was carried out but nothing was found. Over the next few months Mr Noble and his sister-in-law caught glimpses of a similar animal on three occasions. A visitor to his farm brought the carcase of a lamb which he said he'd seen a large cat-like animal drop as it was jumping over the 6ft high forestry fence. They examined the carcase and saw that the head had been almost severed; skinning revealed puncture wounds on both sides of the chest wall which penetrated into the gut. However, the carcase was not examined by the police or a vet.

It was during the spring of 1980 that Miss Chisholm reported a horrible wailing on the hillside above her home. It lasted from about midnight to 5.00am over two nights and sounded like a woman screaming. Other people reported hearing similar sounds.

In late April – early May, at about 8.30pm, a farmer at Cannich was checking his stock on the hillside. In the dusk he spotted an animal making down the field towards his sheep. It noticed him when it was about 100yd from him and then it ran off and disappeared towards the hill. He described the animal as long and low with a long cat-like tail. He did not see its head but its colour appeared to be dark tan with its back lighter than its flanks. The carcases of twelve lambs were also discovered at Cannich. It was impossible to determine how the animals had died, whether they had been still-born or killed, but in each case the carcases had been skinned before being gnawed at in cat fashion.

In June Miss Chisholm received another cat-like visitor near her cottage. But this animal was very different from the black animals she had previously seen. She spotted a bunch of red hinds congregated in a corner of the deer-fence where they had broken it down. Sitting on a post watching them was a dog-sized cat, yellow-coloured with dark-brown markings on its body like rings or stripes. The animal was smaller than either of the black cats that she had seen and she thought it was like a tiger-cub.

21

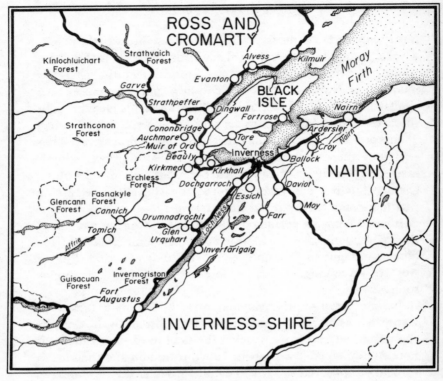

Map 1 Inverness area

The following day she heard screams in the wood and to her amazement saw yet another large cat-like animal crossing the road. This one was plain tan-coloured like a puma or lioness.

At the end of July or beginning of August, three hillwalkers at Glen Affric, near Cannich, heard an unearthly scream coming from the hills. It was unlike anything they had ever experienced before and so terrified them that they fled panic-stricken from the area.

On 28 August, a scientific officer from the Institute of Terrestrial Ecology, Banchory, was collecting birch seeds from the hill area near Mr Ted Noble's farm and directly above and about half a mile from Miss Chisholm's cottage. At 11.00am he was amazed to see an animal in a clearing among the birch and gorse, about 30–40yd away from him. It was sitting with its back to him and his first impression was that it was a huge black cat. He estimated its size as larger than a fully grown Alsatian dog. Its colour was definitely black and it had a long thick tail. The weather was dry and sunny and this eliminated the possibility that the animal's coat appeared black because it was wet. The witness decided that discretion was the order of the day and made a hasty retreat.

But the black cat soon proved it had company. On 11 September Miss Chisholm was again alerted by the commotion her hens were making. On investigating the cause of the trouble she saw a large striped cat crouching low and stalking the hens. She said it was a really beautiful animal with dark-brown stripes on a gold coat; it had a tuft on the end of its tail and was about the size of a dog.

Meanwhile farmer Ted Noble had been laying bait around the hillside in the area of Miss Chisholm's cottage. Some of the bait seemed to have been taken, so he erected a trap with a sprung door that was connected to a sheep's head inside the cage. On 29 October he appeared to have been successful, for he reported having caught a fully grown female puma. However, a lot of controversy still surrounds the capture. The animal, aged about ten years and weighing approximately 80lb, is apparently completely tame. Eddie Orbell, in charge of the Highland Wild Life Park where the animal now is, stated that in his opinion it had never spent so long as thirty minutes in the wild. As one person said at the time, it was just a great big pussy cat that liked its head scratched. It also refused to eat an unskinned rabbit and would only take prepared food. All experts agreed that this puma could not possibly have been responsible for the sheep killing in the area. Also, it had obviously not lactated recently and many reports of sightings had mentioned cub-like animals. The general opinion was that the animal had been put in the trap as an elaborate hoax, but just who was responsible and where the animal has come from is unknown. Detective Sergeant Cathcart knows Mr Noble well and doesn't feel that he was involved, rather that the joke was against him. Whoever was responsible, it certainly wasn't the poor puma that was responsible for the sheep killings or the sightings, for those continued after the friendly animal was securely behind bars. Miss Chisholm stated that although the puma was about the same size as the black animal, she had not seen it before. Other witnesses were also shown the puma; they also agreed that the size was right, but all stated that the colour was not the same as that of the animals they had sighted.

And, in November 1981, mysterious sheep deaths still continued. Over a ten-day period a farmer from Cannich found four of his sheep killed and eaten. The carcases had not been worried by dogs and the manner in which they had been eaten was consistent with the style of a cat-type predator. One sheep had had its neck broken in the attack. A search of the area was made but nothing further was found.

Some 25 miles to the west of the Cannich area, other unknown animals have been reported. On 21 January 1980 part of a sheep carcase was found about 200yd from an isolated house at Strathcarron. The occupiers stated that their dogs had been disturbed and had been barking for the previous three nights.

On 24 July at about 3.00pm an Aberdeen hillwalker was near Achnashellach Forest when he spotted what he thought at first was a stag lying in the heather. However, he realised it was a large cat-like animal when it got up, snarled and then made off into the woods. He described it as about 3½ft long and 2½ft high at the hindquarters. It was fawn in colour and definitely of the cat family.

Just over a year later, in November 1981, two schoolgirls walking to a Brownies meeting near their home at Lochcarron were approached from behind by an animal that sniffed at their legs and then ran off. Although it was fairly dark at the time, both children described the animal as a 'dog with a cat's face'. They were terrified and ran home in a very distressed state.

Another area of sightings is around Loch Ness. Merchant seaman Thomas McMahon was holidaying in Scotland in the spring of 1967, and one evening was hitching along the road between Inverness and Fort Augustus. He said:

> It was starting getting dark and I thought to myself that it was time to make camp. It was still lightish and there was a lot of scrub and heather along the road, when suddenly I saw the glint from these eyes. And I can always remember, even to this day, first thing in my mind was, what the heck is that? It clicked, you know how your mind works fast, 'That's no ordinary cat, or no dog or anything!' It was like a puma with its ears laid back, about the size of a Labrador but not as heavily built. It was the height and build of a leopard. I was walking in the centre of the road and it was standing on the verge, it couldn't have been more than a couple of feet away from me. I thought, if that thing goes for me, well I had a small haversack and I thought that I could use it as a shield, as I didn't know if it was aggressive or not. There was dead silence, the eyes followed me as I passed, I looked back once or twice warily and it was still looking at me. There was an awful sense of awareness, you know, it was not a thing to be tangling with. That's all I can remember. You couldn't tell the colour in the light, it was a sort of darkish grey.

Mrs Sharon Lord was holidaying at Drumnadrochit, Loch Ness, in the summer of 1976, and sat down on a hillside. As she stretched out her arm behind her, to her horror she put her hand on a large cat-like animal that had been lying concealed in the bracken. The animal leapt up, spitting, and bit her hand, the crescent-shaped scar remaining to this day. As she screamed, the animal sprang away and disappeared into the undergrowth. She described it as twice the size of a domestic cat, about the size of a medium dog, orangey-brown in colour with black spots and stripes. It had pricked-up ears with tufts of hair on the end. She didn't see a tail but, as she said, 'I was too busy concentrating on the end with teeth to bother about looking for a tail.'

On a July evening in 1980 a holidaymaker reported seeing a strange cat-like animal on the shores of Loch Ness between Dores and Inverfarigaig. It was chasing three deer, which apparently swam out into the loch and drowned. The witness only saw the rear quarters of the animal but described it as a large cat the size of an Afghan hound, with an arched back and dark grey in colour.

The next sighting in the area was on 4 December, when a motorist driving near Drumnadrochit reported what she described as a lioness. It was about 4ft long with large paws, a fawn coat and a long cat-like tail. The area where the sighting had occurred was examined and an indistinct cat-like spoor was found in the roadside grit. It showed four pads and measured 4in across. At around 3.00pm on 7 December, a man was walking his dog on the banks of the River Enrick at Drumnadrochit when he saw, at about 35yd distance, a tawny-coloured cat-like animal about the size of a Labrador dog. Again an indistinct spoor was found, but it only measured about 3in in diameter, smaller than the other prints. Four days later, at about 2.00am, it was reported that a large cat-like animal had forced open a dustbin at a house near Drumnadrochit.

On 16 March 1981, Lord Burton of the Dochfour Estate found the savaged carcase of a roe deer. Nearby were large cat-like prints that could have been made by an animal the size of a puma. Unfortunately, the prints were erased by the rain before they could be fully examined.

At 2.30pm on 30 August a police driver spotted two animals standing in the roadway as he was driving between Dores and Inverfarigaig on Loch Ness side. He saw them in good light at a distance of about 30yd. The animals were definitely cats and similar in appearance, of a grey colouration with some white about the chest. They stood about 3ft at the head, and he noticed that one had a thick curved tail. On being disturbed both animals ran off very quickly towards the water's edge where he lost sight of them.

The area roughly bounded by Inverness, Beauly, Garve and Black Isle has had many sightings. On 30 January 1979 a lioness-like animal was seen near Bishop Kinkell, Conon Bridge. This animal was carrying a cat in its mouth and it disappeared into a nearby wood, though whether the cat was prey or a cub is unclear from the report. Helen Fitch of Bishop Kinkell watched the animal in a field about 100yd from her house. She said it was 'a big cat, similar to a small lioness or puma. I have lived in

Central Africa and seen animals like that before.' Police took casts of prints. A week later farmer John Henderson reported prints 3–4in across, the pads and claw indentations of which could be clearly seen, just a mile from Mrs Fitch's sighting.

At about 9.50pm on 3 November, the driver of a train travelling from Kyle of Lochalsh to Inverness saw an animal like a lioness near Garve station. At about 1.00am on the following day a large cat-type animal was reported seen at Rogart.

Two days later, in the evening of 6 November, four men in a car saw a lioness in the headlights. The sighting was near Maryburgh, 2 miles from Dingwall. A crofter reported a sheep carcase that appeared to have been eaten.

On 8 November, at about eight in the evening, a lioness was reported seen by a witness in the headlights of his car in the suburbs of Dingwall near the fire station. Five days later a fawn-coloured young lioness was reported at the same place.

At about midday on 12 November, a railway trackman came face to face with a lioness on the railway track 9 miles from Dingwall on the Garve track. The animal seems to have been as unnerved by the encounter as the man. It bounded over a fence and disappeared into woodland. On the same day at about 5.00pm a large cat-like animal was reported in the woodland at Milnafua, Alness, 16 miles from where the railway worker sighted the lioness.

Three days later, at 11.45pm, a civil engineer was driving on the new A9 at Tore roundabout near Dingwall when he saw a cat-like animal. He turned his car around to get a second look. He described it as about 4ft long and 2ft 6in high. It was dark-coloured, lion-like but without a mane, had a long thin tail and small ears; it loped as it ran and looked like a large cat, but was not a wild cat. On 22 November at about 5.40pm, a housewife at Dingwall disturbed a large cat-like animal in her back garden. She described it as light brown in colour, with a round head and large eyes. It was about 2ft 6in high.

At 7.15pm on 23 November, a motorist driving near Strathpeffer spotted a large cat-like animal running across the road. This witness had spent some time in Africa and he was convinced that the animal he had seen was definitely not a lioness. It was the size of a sheep, fawn in colour and had a long springy tail.

On 27 November at about 2.30pm two men were driving near Kiltarlity, south of Beauly, when they saw an animal on the road about 100yd away. It was cat-like with a short golden-yellow coat, a large head and a long tail, and was larger than a fully grown Labrador dog. One witness swore that he'd seen a lioness. The next day a taxi-driver was near Kiltarlity when she caught sight of a large cat-like animal in her car's headlights. It was fawn in colour with a cat-type face and large paws. It had a slim build, long thin tail, and was about 4ft in length and 2ft high.

The new year, 1980, immediately brought further reports. On 16 January a retired gamekeeper reported finding unusual footprints in the snow at South Clunes, just west of Inverness. They measured 7in long by 4in wide and were like nothing he'd ever seen before.

At about 11.30am on 30 January, a Muir of Ord man reported seeing a large dog-sized gold-coloured cat-like animal crossing the railway line and disappearing towards Bishop Kinkell.

On 28 June a housewife reported having seen a large cat-like animal in her garden at Evanton. It was $3\frac{1}{2}$ft long, about 2ft high, and yellowish-coloured with the head of a cat and the body of a dog.

Then on 17 November the remains of two sheep were found on farms 3 miles apart at Garve. The carcases had been cleanly stripped of all muscle and soft organs, and the rib cages had been partially eaten. The contents of the stomach of one of the animals were discovered approximately 80yd from the carcase, but there was no trace of the internal organs. One carcase had been killed during the night, but the other had died about four days earlier. A vet examining the carcases noted the lack of mess around the remains and concluded that the same species of animal had been responsible for both killings, which he could not associate with either dogs or foxes. The carcases were taken to the Institute of Terrestrial Ecology at Banchory, where they were examined by a doctor of zoology and a biologist. They stated that both animals had been killed by a throat bite, one having been suffocated in typical cat fashion, and that they could have been killed and eaten by a large carnivore such as a puma. However, with the usual careful scientific hedging, they went on to state that 'although the patterns of damage were unlikely to have been caused by a fox, dog, wild cat or badger, due to variations, these could not be excluded'. Which translates to my mind that they thought the beasts were killed and eaten by a cat-type predator but they dared not stick their necks out and say so.

On 30 November a crofter at Garve discovered another sheep carcase. It had been completely devoured and all that remained was the head, fleece and part of the rib cage and spine. The contents of the stomach sac were found about 15yd from the remains. The carcase was examined by a vet, and although he could not give the exact cause of death, he noted very close similarities between it and the other two. There was a large hole in the animal's throat.

And at 8.00am on 16 December 1981, a motorist who was driving near South Clunes, saw a large cat-like animal crossing the road. It was tan-coloured, about the size of a Labrador dog, and had a long thick tail. It jumped the fence before disappearing into woodland. The witness was certain it was a puma. Although there was snow on the ground, it had frozen so hard that the animal left no tracks.

South of the Moray Firth, on 29 September 1977 Mr John Jenkins, together with his son and nephew, spotted a lioness with two cubs at 5.30pm. They watched the animals from a distance of about 20ft in a field at Crask, Farr, 10 miles south of Inverness. The following day a similar sighting was reported from near Culduthel, Inverness. Later a report was received by the police that two witnesses had seen three cub-like animals about 5 miles from Farr. The animals were seen in the car's headlights and described as grey in colour with short cat-like faces. The witnesses were both country-bred and stated that the animals were definitely not wild cats, foxes or badgers.

At about 8.00pm on 21 November 1979, a large cat-like animal was reported seen at Daviot. It was 6ft long and 2½ft high, with a cat-like head, a short coat and a bushy tail.

The next reported sighting was by an off-duty policeman. On 12 October 1980 at 3.20am he was driving between Inverness and Nairn when he saw a large cat-like animal on the road. It was a grey or fawny-tan colour and about 4ft long with another 2ft of tail. It had short fur and a cat's head. He believed it was a puma. The animal was running very quickly in a smooth leaping action and crossed the road in about two bounds.

At about 6.20pm on 19 October, an Inverness woman motorist was travelling from Inverarnie to Daviot when she saw a large cat-like animal by the roadside. It was a fairly bright night and visibility was excellent. She described it as slightly taller and longer than an adult Labrador dog, but slightly slimmer in build. It was yellow-fawn in colour all over, the head was round with a short face and the tail was much longer in proportion to its body than that of a dog of the same size. It moved very gracefully, like a cat.

At 5.30am on 25 July 1981, a workman coming off shift at the oil-platform construction site at Ardersier spotted some crows feeding on the carcase of a dead rabbit that was lying at the side of the access road to the site. He slowed down, and when he was about 15yd from the carcase an animal came out of the undergrowth and crossed the road. He described it as larger than an Alsatian dog, with short legs, large paws and a thick tail. It was tan-coloured and identical to a puma. At 8.50pm the following day a woman motorist was driving on the same access road when she saw a large lioness-type animal feeding on a dead rabbit at the side of the road. She described it as larger than a Labrador dog and yellow-brown in colour with a long thick tail.

Besides Inverness-shire and Ross and Cromarty, another part of Scotland to produce a large number of big-cat reports over the years is Sutherland. The first sighting to be recorded and taken notice of by the police was in the Strathnaver area in 1975. A police sergeant on holiday was driving in the strath with three passengers when an animal like a puma suddenly leapt out in front of the car. It bounded across the road carrying a rabbit in its mouth and with one apparently effortless leap cleared a 9ft high forestry fence. Reports of other sightings slowly came in.

In the winter a crofter and his wife were working on their land overlooking the River Naver one afternoon when they spotted a large cat-type animal about the size of a big collie dog. It came out of the woods on the west bank and swam across the river. They watched it for several minutes from a distance of about 200yd.

In 1976 crofters in the area began to notice unusual sheep and chicken losses. As one crofter told local policeman Keith Hart, it was usual to lose one or two sheep but he'd lost sixteen. A number of people in the Strathnaver and Bettyhill areas reported sightings of a large black or dark brown cat-like animal.

Hugh Mackay, a crofter who had lost a number of sheep, and local milkman Alistair McLean were out shooting foxes when they saw a large animal running across the moors. Mr McLean said, 'It was broad in the back, strongly built and very fast. I thought it was a dull rusty colour and was convinced it was big game.' In January 1977 sheep losses became worse in the Skerray area, just 2 miles from Bettyhill. A local roads foreman, Mr Crow, complained about the number of sheep he was losing and Alistair McLean agreed to help him hunt the animal responsible. Carrying a .22 rifle and a 12-bore shotgun, they went up into the hills at Torrisdale where the sheep had been disappearing. After a few hours they suddenly disturbed a large cat-like animal that leapt out of a peat trench in front of them and bounded away over the rise of the hill. Although they gave chase, the animal moved at tremendous speed and was soon out of range. It was a cat, black-coloured, larger than a collie dog and with a long bushy tail.

At the end of November 1977 the local storekeeper at Achneiskich, Thomas Todd, found the carcase of one of his sheep in the park at the rear of his croft. He stated: 'I had never seen anything like it, the skin was removed as cleanly as if it had been professionally flayed. Absolutely all the flesh had been removed and many of the bones including the upper parts of the legs and jaw were missing. The backbone and skull were there but the ribs had been chewed right into the vertebrae. There was very little sign of a struggle so whatever killed the sheep did so very quickly and efficiently.' The remains were sent to the Veterinary Research Laboratory in Thurso where they were examined by the Veterinary Investigation Officer, W. Scott Johnston. He said: 'In my opinion the killing was the work of a member of the cat family. There is no conclusive proof but the neatness of the kill, the spacing of the toothmarks and the crushing of the bones all point to a feline predator.' He added that it would have needed to be a fairly large animal to have made the kill. Mr Todd told how he had earlier found tracks in the snow with paw-prints measuring 3in in diameter.

A few days later, Donald Mackenzie and his son James were out lamping for foxes. On the shoreline by Bettyhill, on the east side of the River Naver, they spotted a large cat-like animal in the lamp beam. The animal seemed to race towards them and Mr Mackenzie fired with a .22 rifle. The creature rolled as though it had been hit and then regained its feet, jumped a wall and made its escape across the river. The following day a thorough search of the area was made in case the animal was wounded and therefore dangerous. There was no sign of it, but cat-like tracks were found in the mud. These measured 3in in diameter. A further search revealed eight more carcases identical to the one found by Mr Todd but in varying stages of decomposition.

In late January–early February, George Mackay, a crofter from Swordly near Bettyhill, complained that his family had heard the most weird screeching noises coming from the hill behind his cottage. He was familiar with the normal country sounds and was convinced that the noises weren't made by foxes or owls. He was certain it was a cat. Policeman Keith Hart from Strathnaver and Police Constable Gunn from Tongue, about 15

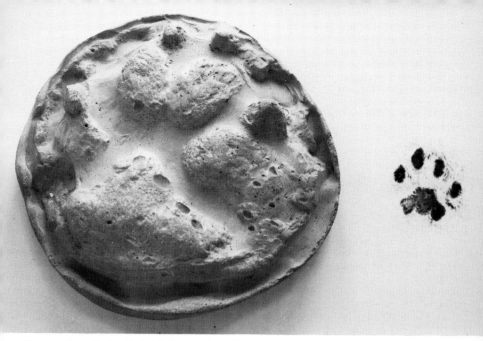

Cast made at Stoke Gabriel, Devon (see Chapter 2) and photographed next to the front paw print of a domestic cat (*Jonathon Bosley*)

Cast made at Tedbury St Mary, Devon, and photographed next to the front paw print of a domestic cat (*Jonathon Bosley*)

Cast made at Tonmawr, Wales (see Chapter 5) and photographed with the front paw print of a domestic cat. Both are shown here actual size (*Jonathon Bosley*)

miles to the west, decided to mount a hunting party. As the group
of local farmers and police were getting ready, a woman motorist
reported seeing a large puma-like animal on the coast road about
10 miles east of Bettyhill. On the road towards Baligill, the group
that included policeman Keith Hart spotted a large black cat, the
size of a fully grown Labrador dog. It moved off in an effortless
smooth lope, rapidly losing its hunters. Its eyes showed up as a
yellowy-blue in the lamp light. The group had two more
sightings of the animal but never managed to get a shot at it.
The following day a search was undertaken by armed police
marksmen and gamekeepers but there was no sign of it.

A few weeks later another sheep carcase was examined by Mr
Scott Johnston and once more he confirmed that it was the work
of a large cat-like predator. Police Sergeant Donald Bruce said:
'There now seems to be a pattern over a wide area which suggests
there could be more than one animal. It is very difficult to find
the animal because it kills at night. When we had snow, tracks
were found but we were unable to follow them because we were
busy digging people out of the snow.' You can appreciate
Sergeant Bruce's feelings when you consider that over a two-
year period the police had received forty reliable sightings,
including a number from members of the force, and about eighty
sheep had been reported taken by the animal. However, the
bewilderment and helplessness felt by Sergeant Bruce were
shared by policemen all over the British Isles.

Still in Scotland, during the summer of 1974 there were a
number of reports that puma-like animals had been seen in north
Ayrshire, south-west of Glasgow. In June, John Jackson, a taxi-
driver from Barrmill, was driving with passengers to Beith at
about midnight. Suddenly he spotted a large cat-like animal
crouched in the road. 'It was sitting on its haunches in the middle
of the road and I was forced to stop. I was within a few feet of it
and my headlights were full on, but it would not move. I waited
for about five minutes, then drove round it. In doing so my car
brushed against it and it growled.' The same month Hugh
Gilmour, a lorry driver, also from Barrmill, was driving early

one morning when he was startled to see a large cat-like animal bound across the road in front of him. He said: 'Its body was $2\frac{1}{2}$ to 3ft from the ground, it had heavy legs, fairly large paws and a long curled-up tail.' He described the animal as lion-like.

By August 1976 the sightings in the Glasgow area numbered over a hundred, including about twenty from policemen. John Stewart, a farmer at Ballgeich Hill 8 miles south of the city, found five dead geese on his land. Each had $1\frac{1}{2}$in deep puncture marks on the body about 4—5in apart. The 6ft wire fence of the enclosure had been ripped open and an Alsatian was cowering nearby. Richard O'Grady, a director of Calderpark Zoo, identified large tracks found nearby as cat-like; he also felt that the puncture marks on the geese were consistent with an attack by a large puma-like predator.

I spoke to Calderpark Zoo in the autumn of 1981. The big cats were still being reported and a spokesman told me that the situation was giving them so many headaches that it had been suggested that someone should be officially appointed by the government to deal directly with all big-cat sightings in Scotland. In 1981 they were receiving reports of yet another animal in the Edinburgh area.

And it certainly wasn't an American puma seen in Perthshire on 9 August 1976. A Glenfarg woman heard her terrier dog yelping in the garden. When she went to investigate what was disturbing the dog she was confronted by a large cat-like creature sitting on top of the wall. It had eyes of burning orange and long pointed ears with tufts on the tips, and it spat and snarled at her as the terrier shivered with fright. With remarkable courage, the lady snatched her dog to safety and backed into the house. The huge cat leapt from the wall and made off into the fields on the other side.

England

In Yorkshire on the same day, 9 August 1976, as the lady in Glenfarg had to rescue her dog, Alan Pestell, a 33-year-old electrical supervisor from Thorganby, was walking along the main road at about 10.00pm when, from the shadows, came a large animal. Mr Pestell said, 'At first I thought it was a dog and spoke to it, but then I realised it had a cat's face and a long tail! I was scared stiff. I froze for a few seconds and then decided to keep on walking to the pub. I thought if I turned and ran it might jump on my back.' He described it as 3–4ft long and nearly 3ft high and said that it sat and looked at him with its right paw lifted until he passed. Then it returned to the shadows and Mr Pestell continued to the local for a much-needed drink.

A few days earlier, on 29 July 1976, two milkmen were on their round at 6.00am at Tollerton, 4 miles south-east of Nottingham. David Bently of Bridgford suddenly spotted a lion-like animal. His mate, David Crowther of Clifton, joined him and together they watched it. Mr Crowther said, 'We both saw together what certainly to us was a lion. It was fifty yards away, had its head down and its long tail had a bushy end. It was walking away from us but only very slowly.' Mr Bently said, 'If I had been on my own I don't think I would have believed it. But it was there and we both saw it together.' A farmer at Clipston near Cotgrave reported strange cat-like paw-prints on his land. The publicity that followed the sighting brought forward another eighteen sightings of large lion-like animals that had occurred before the milkmen's encounter.

On 31 July a farmer, John Dunthorne, spotted a large lion-like cat on his farm and later found tracks. In the evening of 1 August, Dr John Chisholm, the deputy coroner for Nottinghamshire, saw the rear end of what appeared to be a lion breaking through the undergrowth to get to a stream in the garden of his home at Normanton on the Wolds. He watched the animal with his wife and 18-year-old son, but the arrival of a police car disturbed it and it made off. The same day, but 10 miles away from Normanton at Nuthall, a woman watched a large puma-like cat stalking wildfowl by a reservoir. She studied the animal through binoculars from a distance of about 200yd.

By 5 August, when it was reported that a sandy-coloured animal like a young lioness had been seen in a field near Nottingham racecourse, the police had received sixty-five reports of sightings. Although some could be discounted, they took a great many seriously. Yet despite searches by hundreds of men and armed police they drew a blank. Checks with the local zoos and wildlife parks showed all animals accounted for. The Nottinghamshire Constabulary felt just as bewildered as Sergeant Bruce in Sutherland.

The following month gave another member of the constabulary cause for thought. At Skegness in Lincolnshire, the staff of a sea-front convalescent home had on a number of occasions, over a period of weeks, seen a large cat-like animal in the grounds. On 20 September Dr Alec Jamieson, a police surgeon, watched the animal with Police Constable Jock Gartshore. Dr Jamieson said that 'It was a large sandy-coloured cat about 5ft long, definitely a cougar.' Pug-marks were found measuring 2½in by 3in. A watch was kept, but the animal seemed to sense danger and stayed away.

On 23 October another lion was seen – this time in Deva Lane at Upton in Cheshire. The sighting was only about a mile away from Chester Zoo, so it seemed there was a rather obvious explanation. However, a check revealed all big and little cats accounted for. Two more reports of the animal were received from the area of West Chester Hospital, but despite an immediate police search, nothing was found.

The police in Norfolk would have been sympathetic towards their colleagues in Nottinghamshire, Lincolnshire and Cheshire. In February 1964 they had received a large number of reports from East Runton near Cromer. Witnesses reported seeing large cat-like animals in the area of the railway embankment. However, to confuse the poor police totally, the sightings were varied – the animals were described as spotted, striped and plain-coloured, and were said to be lion-like, tiger-like, puma-like and even cheetah-like. The police search revealed nothing. Then on 15 January 1975 a lorry driver reported seeing two lion cubs playing around the council tip at Langham. Council rodent-control officer Bill Crane investigated but found nothing.

In 1964 Oxfordshire joined the 'big cat territory' counties when sightings of a large cat-like animal in woods near Nettlebed were reported. In the next-door county, Buckinghamshire, on 12 November that year, two policemen reported seeing a large cat-like animal near the poet Thomas Gray's memorial at Stoke Poges.

But these two counties couldn't keep up with Berkshire, Surrey and Hampshire. Berkshire is a county of small woods and gentle hills, very different from the wilds of Scotland. Its most striking area of natural beauty is the Vale of White Horse. At Crowthorne on Bagshot Heath, close to the Surrey and Hampshire borders, is Wellington College; around and within the college grounds there have been a number of large-cat sightings during recent years. Unfortunately it wasn't until 1981 that the police began to take notice of the witnesses who described such sightings, but once the authorities did take an interest, they followed up all reports with care. Like Detective Sergeant Cathcart in Scotland, Sergeant John Gregson took a personal interest, and witnesses were interviewed, statements were taken and police patrols kept watch around the college. The following eyewitness statements were taken from either personal interviews or police files. For this reason I have not used full names or addresses unless I have received permission, but it is worth repeating that every signed statement taken by the police bears the warning that the writer shall be liable to prosecution if it is tendered in evidence and the writer has knowingly made a false statement.

In June 1981 a teacher at the college was exercising his Irish setter at 9.50pm in the grounds of the estate when he spotted a fox-like animal crouched in the grass about 100yd from him. When the animal saw him it got up, turned in a tight circle and took off at 'an amazing speed', taking about twelve seconds to cover about 150yd. He was amazed by the sinuous way in which the creature moved, both hind and front legs meeting each other in a bounding action. It was about the size of a setter and reddish-brown in colour with a distinctly long tail. He was convinced that the animal was not a dog, but of the cat family. He reported his sighting to the police. I have a letter from him describing his experience, but owing to the adverse press publicity he is adamant that he will not have his letter reproduced, and therefore I have not used his name or quoted him in full.

However, this gentleman was not alone in seeing a large cat-like animal in this district. A couple, Mr and Mrs Paternoster, were walking in the same area, just 300yd from the scene of the teacher's sighting, when they saw a jet-black cat the size of a Great Dane. They watched it from a distance of about 20yd.

On 2 July a student at the college, aged fourteen, was with friends:

> At 11.38am on Thursday 2nd July 1981, I was in the English Form in Queen's Court at Wellington College. I saw two friends on the patio looking down towards the pond. I went out and joined them and saw an animal sitting in front of a tree about one hundred metres away from me. My two friends set off towards it and I followed on behind.
>
> The animal was within my view all the time, not moving, until my two friends got to within thirty metres of it. I was ten metres behind them. I then saw it move very fast, forty-five degrees to its right, and disappear into the undergrowth and bushes. I would describe it as being as large as a Labrador dog whilst it was sitting. It was jet black in colour with a very smooth, glossy coat with short hair. When it moved I would estimate its length from head to rear of body, excluding tail which I did not notice, was four feet. It looked in very good condition and was fit. In moving very fast it seemed to take long strides. I am adamant that it was not a domestic cat or dog, it was a very large feline animal but I do not know what breed.
>
> I had learned that there had been one or two sightings of an animal recently and that there had been something on TV but I did not see the item nor have I read anything about it in the press. The weather was fine and dry, visibility was very good, cloudy but bright. I am certain of what I saw and would recognise it again.

The second statement is by one of the other boys who saw the animal. Again he was aged fourteen.

40

About 11.38am on Thursday 2nd July I was on a patio at the rear of Queen's Court, Wellington College, waiting for a lesson to start, amongst other students. Something was said which caused me to look across the pond towards some trees about 100yds away. I saw a black silhouette in front of the trees, I was curious and walked down the slope towards it.

It remained in my view all the time and as I got nearer it got larger, I knew it was an animal and I had heard reports of a puma being in the grounds. I got to within twenty-five yards of the animal when I saw that it was sat upright, its rear legs being folded under its body. Its head was turned away from us and its body was side on to us. Its head turned towards us, it saw us and bolted away into the undergrowth behind it. It did not make any sound except the rustle of the undergrowth.

I would describe it as being a shiny black colour, I did not see its whole body side on, but when it sat up I would estimate that its head was two foot six inches from the ground. Its head was rounded, with short pointed ears which looked white inside. It looked well fed and in very good condition. When it moved it turned very sharply and moved very fast.

The weather was clear and fine, visibility was very good, my eyesight is very good. I am convinced of what I saw, this is not a hoax. The animal did not look like any dog or cat that I have ever seen, it sat like a cat and it moved very fast. I am convinced that it was a largish wild cat.

I have not seen or read any newspaper or television reports on the subject, although there has been talk around the school. I am aware of the penalties of making a false report.

If the final lines of the statement were a plea for adults to believe him, four days later the boys had at least one supporter. On 6 July a local shopkeeper came forward with the following statement:

About 8.00pm on Thursday 2nd July 1981, I was walking along the footpath which leads from Dukes Ride to Wellington College squash courts with my dog. On my right was a very large field which was covered in grass 9–12 inches long in places. The grass is uneven and in places flattened.

I turned off the path and walked along the edge of the woods for about 50–60 yards. On reaching this point I looked across the field and about 40 yards away I saw a black shape in the grass. I recognised it as being an animal. I saw that it was lying down and that its head was to my left. I saw that the head was as large as a ten-year-old child's, the ears were in proportion to the head and they were pointed. It looked like a very large cat. I could also see the line of its back and hindquarters, also its tail.

The tail was almost as long as its body. It did not move at all. The most noticeable feature was its bright red eyes, they almost seemed to flash — as if they were lit by a battery. I estimate that the total length of the animal from head to tail, whilst lying down, was about 4 feet. I watched it for about five minutes but did not approach it.

The weather was fine and dry and the sun was setting in the west, behind the animal. Visibility was excellent, my eyesight with glasses, which I was wearing, is very good.

I went home, left my dog and collected my binoculars and returned to the same spot but the animal was gone. I was only away about six minutes. The only thing I saw on my return was three youths cycling across the field, near to the spot where the animal had been, towards Wellington College from the direction of the railway station. I do not know if they had anything to do with it but I recollect hearing noises in the woods prior to my sighting. I am adament about what I saw but I do not know if it was real or not.

Police patrols having been sent to the area because of the reported sightings, Police Constable Urvoy also heard sounds. He said:

At 1345 hours on Thursday 2nd July, I was on duty in uniform in the grounds of Wellington College, Crowthorne. At this time I was walking along a tarmacadam road I know to be Back Drive. There is thick woodland on both sides of the road.

I heard the sound of what I would describe to be a large wild cat snarling to my right slightly ahead of me. I did not see any animal and another Officer and myself made a search of the area with a negative result.

There seems little doubt that a large black cat-like animal was roaming the woods on 2 July and that this was similar to the animal seen by Mr and Mrs Paternoster, but it certainly was not the animal seen by the teacher. For that was fox- or reddish-brown coloured. However a few days later a retired couple out walking reported seeing a large cat in Crowthorne Woods. But it wasn't described as reddish-brown, it was brown.

The husband made the following statement:

At about 3pm on Thursday 9th July 1981, together with my wife, I
was out walking my dog along a fire-track in the Crowthorne
Woods, Crowthorne. This track runs practically parallel to the
A3095 Crowthorne road. We had walked for a distance of about a
quarter of a mile from the Devil's Highway. As we were just coming
over a slight brow of a hill, I saw at about 40 yards in front of me,
almost directly in front, what I can only describe as a female lioness,
walking across the track in the distinctive sway of a cat, in a slow
graceful movement. I would say that this lion was bigger than an
Alsatian, full grown, it had a smooth brown-gold coat.
It had a 2 foot-long tail with a brush at the end. It was a lion,
there was absolutely no doubt about it in my mind. I was shocked by
the sight of it and by the time I recovered and had said to my wife
'Christ, there's a lion' my wife was next to me, but she wasn't
looking straight ahead initially until I mentioned it. The lion by that
time had entered the bracken on my right. The lion seemed in no
hurry and had merely ambled across, I'm not sure if it saw us. My
next reaction was to turn back immediately and quickly report the
matter to the police. I've seen lions several times in the past, in the
wild and on television, so I know what a lion looks like. I would like
to mention that there was a stream running within twenty yards
from where it crossed and I would assume it had been there for a
drink prior to our presence. I fully understand the implications of
making a false statement to the police but would not have reported
it unless I was absolutely sure.

One can only feel that there was much emotion behind those
erse words to his wife! She agreed with his description of the
nimal:

At about 3pm on Thursday 9th July 1981, I was out walking with
my husband and our dog, along a fire-track in the Crowthorne
Woods. We had walked from the Devil's Highway in Crowthorne
into the woodland. We had travelled for about a quarter of a mile
and I recall going over a slight brow of a hill. I was walking with my
head down at that point, when my husband said 'Christ, there's a
lion!' I immediately looked ahead along the track and I could see the
back of what I would say was a lion. It was bigger than an Alsatian,
it was a gold-brown colour, with a short coat. I couldn't see its tail or
its head. It didn't appear to be in any hurry. I only saw it for a few
seconds and that is all I can recall about it. The colouring convinced

43

me that it was a lion. When I saw it, it was from a distance of 30 to 40 yards. I realise and fully understand the implications of making a false statement to the police.

No doubt the lady did. But one can understand the confusion that members of the local constabulary were feeling: a black panther, a reddish-brown puma and now a lion! And a very young lion, if it really wasn't much bigger than an Alsatian dog. After all, Alsatians weigh about 70lb, but lions weigh upwards of 300lb. They make Great Danes look small. But why should all these perfectly respectable people make lying statements to the police? And if they were lying, why didn't they all claim to have seen the same creature? And if they weren't lying, they certainly couldn't all have seen the same animal but have been mistaken over minor details. Shaken witnesses are notoriously unreliable in their descriptions, but the colours were too varied for minor changes of light and shade. Yet commonsense refuses to accept the possibility that there was a whole menagerie of escaped big cats in Crowthorne Woods.

On 11 July, four people were strolling through the grounds of Wellington College. They were a teacher from Wellington College – not the same gentleman who had had the original sighting – his wife and his parents. They all saw a large, dark brown cat-like animal. On 8 August, the teacher and his wife made statements to the police:

At about 5.30pm on Saturday 11th July 1981, I was with my wife and my parents, walking along Farm Lane, in the grounds of Wellington College. It was a warm sunny day and visibility was good. To our right and through the trees were the houses of Connaught Close and to the left was an open farm field. At a point approximately 150 yards from the railway bridge, which was just directly in front of us and leads into the Ambarrow Woods, I saw a large cat-like animal, walking along the footpath. It stopped momentarily and looked at us for a few seconds. I could see that it was very dark coloured with a short coat. It was a very thin animal and it had definite cat-like features. It had a long tail which was down towards the ground, but curled at the end. I would say that the animal, apart from thinness, was comparable to a full-grown

Alsatian. I didn't really have time to look at the face, because it moved off towards the bridge and away from us in a fairly quick movement in a very smooth way, similar to a domestic cat. My father and I left the two women and went to the spot where we had seen it, but couldn't find it anywhere. I am fully aware of the consequences of making a false report to the police.

His wife told a similar story:

At about 5pm on Saturday 11 July 1981, I was out walking with my husband and his parents in the grounds of Wellington College. At that time it was fine and sunny, visibility was good. We were walking along a lane which I know as Sewage Farm Lane, this lane carries on into Ambarrow Woods. At a point approximately 100 to 150 yards in front of us, near to the railway bridge just prior to the Ambarrow Woods, I saw a large cat. This animal had walked out from a small lane, near to the bridge, onto the footpath directly in front of us. It paused for a matter of seconds on the footpath. I could see that this cat was dark brown in colour, it had a short coat. It had a very thin build and was very sleek in appearance. There was no doubt in my mind whatsoever that this was a large cat. I have no idea what a puma looks like, as I have never seen one, but this animal was definitely not a domestic cat. It had a long tail which curled at the end in a loop. I would say that the tail was two-thirds the length of its body. It moved in a cat-like gait; it was not a dog of any description, but it was certainly a very large cat. I would say that it was about the size of a red-setter dog. It moved away as my husband started to approach it and crossed the bridge in a quick movement. The hindquarters were obviously like a cat and it moved in a slinking manner. I am fully aware of the consequences of making a false report to the police.

Both schoolteachers could have seen the same animal: they both describe it as setter-sized and brown, although one gives the colour as dark, the other as reddish-brown. But it certainly isn't the same as the jet-black animal or the gold-brown lion.

Crowthorne isn't alone in providing Berkshire people with sightings of large cats. Mr Neville of Ascot, a few miles from Crowthorne, wrote me the following letter:

On Friday 23rd of October at twelve noon, I went to the lake which is hidden amongst thick rhododendrons on a large country estate for the purpose of checking the water level and also looking for the wild

Canada geese etc which visit the lake. When I cautiously crept up to peer through the shrubs, I was shocked and amazed to see a large beautiful jet-black cat-like animal drinking at the clearing. It was a very powerful-looking beast around four to five feet in length, with raised shoulders, a thick neck and a beautiful shiny black coat. It appeared to be aware of my presence at once and as it glanced in my direction, I saw it had large yellowy-green eyes. Suddenly it dashed off through the bushes and left me astounded and as scared as the animal itself!

The letter continues to explain that the writer had previously lived in the Kumoan Hills in northern India and had hunted the panther in the past, so is well aware of the differences between a large cat and any other animal. He mentions that a colleague had also sighted the creature at Bagshot. And in June 1972 Edna Hughes of Bagshot looked out of her window early one morning and found herself looking at a strange cat-like animal that 'slowly walked up and down, staring at me. It was white and about 3 feet high when it sat up.' This sighting was reported in the *Aldershot News* on 23 June 1972. These last two sightings occurred in Surrey, not Berkshire — but the border of the two counties runs directly across Bagshot Common.

The county of Surrey is mostly rural, with large stretches of wooded commons and agricultural land. Most of the recorded sightings have occurred in the Godalming area, which has comparatively large areas of woodland and is fairly hilly, rising to just over 900ft above sea-level. The first record of an unusual cat sighting in Surrey appears in *Rural Rides* by William Cobbett, published in 1830. In the section where he writes about the stretch between Chilworth and Winchester, he tells of seeing a strange cat-like creature in the grounds of Waverley Abbey, near Farnham. Writing on Thursday 27 October he says that as a boy he had spotted a cat as big as a middle-sized spaniel dog, which went up into a hollow elm tree. On telling his family of his sighting he received a scolding and then a beating for insisting he had seen an unidentifiable animal. He adds, 'I have since many times repeated it and I would take my oath of it to this day. When in New Brunswick I saw the great wild grey cat, which is there called a Lucifee, and it seemed to me to be just such a cat as I had seen at Waverley.'

This was much quoted during the so-called 'Surrey puma' sightings of the 1960s. It was supposed to be the first recorded sighting of the puma, for people have claimed that the cat referred to as a 'Lucifee' by Cobbett was indeed an American puma. However, I believe that Cobbett was describing not the puma but that other wild cat of North America, the lynx. A puma would surely be described as brown or tawny, not grey, whereas the lynx does indeed frequently have a thick grey coat. The Canadian lynx has a silver or pinkish-grey coat with smoky markings, perhaps the most beautiful fur of all the lynx family. However, the first public concern regarding large-cat sightings in the Surrey area was during that 1960s period, when police and experts believed that a puma was roaming the countryside. Despite large-scale searches and enormous publicity, the animal was never caught and not even clearly photographed. And yet a number of people claimed to have seen it.

A few reports had been made during the 1950s of encounters with large cats in the Surrey–Hampshire border area – again, the animal is hardly likely to respect a county boundary. Unfortunately records weren't kept, as the stories were treated as either a joke or a hoax. But on the morning of 16 July 1962 Ernest Jellett, an employee of the Mid-Wessex Water Board, went to inspect Heathy Park Reservoir on the North Downs at Farnham. He was walking along a track through a densely wooded area when he saw a large cat-like animal stalking a rabbit. The rabbit, panicking, blundered towards the cat which pounced and missed. Then both animals ran towards where Mr Jellett was standing, and the rabbit escaped into the undergrowth. However the cat bounded straight towards Mr Jellett, who shouted to frighten it away. The cat then made off into the woods. He later described the animal as 'like a young lion cub. It stood about two feet high, was sandy coloured and had a sort of round flat face like a big cat and its tail was long and thin, not bushy. It had big paws.'

Later in 1962 the station superintendent for the Water Board, L. Noble, also reported seeing the animal. And a woman was walking near the village of Crondall when she spotted a large cat-like animal in a field; she later identified it as being like the South American cat, the jaguarundi. Unfortunately at the date of writing I have been unable to trace the lady to ask for more details, but probably the cat she saw was either reddish-brown or dark grey as these are the common colours of the jaguarundi.

In 1964 nearby Farnham became cat-conscious. During the summer, people reported seeing cat-like creatures around Farnham and Bordon. Others reported hearing a frightful howling or weird screaming at night, described by one person as being like 'the sound of a hundred cats being murdered'. According to police files, one man who had both seen and heard a cat-like animal for over two years was farm manager Edward Blanks of Bushylease Farm at Crondall. In August 1964 something stampeded a herd of bullocks which broke out of their field, and later one was found alive but injured in the nearby woods. A vet examining the animal was of the opinion that it had been bitten and mauled by something other than a dog. The steer recovered, but the hunt for the big cat had begun in earnest. Billy Davidson, a Canadian ranger holidaying in Britain, offered his services and Bushylease Farm became the hunt head-quarters. However, although Mr Davidson did find evidence that a big cat was around, the so-called Surrey puma remained at large; not unseen, however, as more and more reports came in.

On 3 September that year, George Wisdom decided to spend his lunch hour picking blackberries on Munstead Heath near Godalming. He was near the Water Tower when he disturbed a large cat-like animal on the other side of a bush. It snarled and spat at him and Mr Wisdom, forgetting any thoughts of blackberries, took to his heels and ran. He described it as having a large cat-like face and being about 3ft high and 5ft long, excluding the long tail. It was a dirty brown-gold colour with short stocky legs and large paws.

Four days later the Godalming police were called to a track at

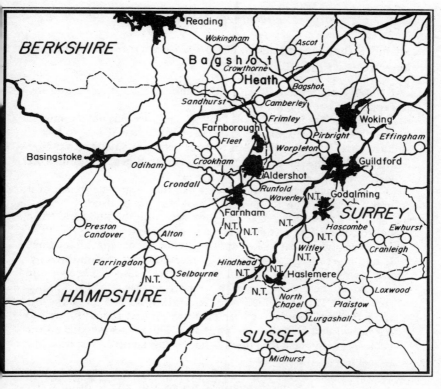

Map 2 'Surrey Puma' Country

Stilemans, Munstead. There on a wide firm sandy surface, sometime between 9.00am and 4.00pm, had appeared a trail of paw-prints stretching uninterrupted for about half a mile. There was no sign of human prints, but the animal prints had been made by a large heavy animal; they were in groups of four and measured $5\frac{1}{2}$in by $5\frac{1}{2}$in. They ended about 2yd from a 5ft 6in high chain-link fence. Hard earth surrounded the base of the fence and would not have shown prints, so it was assumed that the animal had leapt over it and entered the wood. Casts were taken of the prints, which experts couldn't positively identify, although they could have been made by a big cat.

Mrs Christabel Arnold of Crondall often walked near Bushylease Farm land and she observed a large cat-like animal on more than one occasion. In 1981 she wrote the following letter to the *Post Dispatch*:

> I think I have been closer to this animal than anyone and my experience is on police records.
>
> I think it was in the sixties. I say the creature was not a puma. It was the width of Redlands Lane away and I saw it face to face. I have never seen anything quite like it before or since and we have travelled to look at circuses and zoos and seen heaps of pumas big and small.
>
> This animal was not in the least like that. I got the stench of it first a long way up the lane and thought 'fox or deer'.
>
> When I came upon it, it had gone back into the wood and left a half-eaten bird at a stile on my side of the road.
>
> I froze and we just looked at one another, then it spat all the time. It had marks like a cheetah on its face and was greyish, browny-beige with spots and stripes. Its back was deep red-brown and massive at the back legs, which were striped black and red-brown right down. It had a white, beige and grey front and this is the one thing that makes me say it wasn't a puma – it had a beautiful striped red-brown and beigy white-tipped tail. The stripes were as on the back legs with black thin lines. It had yellow slanted eyes, wire-like whiskers and tufted ears.
>
> Afterwards I thought it could have been a lynx. It leapt the width of the lane and went through the hedge, stopping to drink water spilled from the cattle trough. I saw it on several occasions in the distance at the dew pond in the same field, and lying on the air-raid shelter which used to be at Bushylease Farm.
>
> My two dogs went mad when it was anywhere around and one day my husband and I saw five foxes sitting outside the wood – we guessed the creature was inside.
>
> I had a zoo keeper visit me after my sighting but could not identify the animal from all his books, although it was very like a bobcat from Canada. Fortunately it seemed as frightened of me as I was of it (I was petrified!). My legs just turned to jelly. Well one doesn't usually meet up with such things on a country walk.

A policeman informed me that Mrs Arnold's statement was the clearest description he had ever known a witness give. It was no doubt helped by the fact that she did see the animal more than once, and with all the publicity given at the time to the so-called Surrey puma hunt she made a point of really studying the

Classic carcase showing the method of killing and eating prey

Drawing by Reginald Bass from eye-witness reports, showing a puma head on a leopard body

Author's pictures of the black cat in Tonmawr, Wales (see Chapter 5)

The picture below gives a rough idea of scale. The cat is in the centre, slightly above and behind the tree to the left. The marked distance under the arched branch measures $3\frac{1}{2}$ ft

creature. A neighbour of hers, Leonard Hobbs of Marsh Farm, often heard the animal's screams at night, and he once caught sight of it in his car's headlights.

The apparent centre of the puma sightings was the area around Bushylease Farm. After the incident of the mauled 4cwt bullock, Mr Blanks found the remains of a 90lb calf which had been dragged or carried over three fields, away from a neighbour's farm. Then on the night of 22 September 1964 a heifer was found badly clawed in a field at Hindhead. Its injuries were consistent with it having been attacked by a large cat-type predator.

The following afternoon a group of building workers and police officers watched a very large cat-like animal lying in the sun on the slope of a hill at Hascombe. They studied the creature at a distance of about 300yd through binoculars and it seemed to be puma-like. Two police officers attempted to approach it but it made off into the woods leaving behind the fresh remains of a rabbit. At about 7.20pm on 23 September a farm worker reported seeing a puma-like animal walking across a ploughed field in the Cranleigh area. That afternoon a local man heard a cat-like screech in woods near Hascombe. Deer at a water-hole were observed to be chased by something. Later an official of the Zoological Society and police officers examined a deer carcase that appeared to have been savaged by a large predator. On the same day a dead roe deer was found mauled and with a broken neck at Cranleigh. Two days later a man was driving his Land Rover along a road at Dunsfold when a large cat-like animal ran across the road in front of his vehicle. It was about 5–6ft long, 3ft high and a gingery-brown colour.

In all, from 27 September to 18 October, ten people reported seeing puma-like animals in the Cranleigh, Guildford, Hindhead area. On one occasion the animal jumped up into a tree, and an official of the Zoological Society was called in to examine the tree trunk; he found the claw-marks to be similar to those of a puma-type cat.

In the Lurgashall area on 24 October a dead sheep was

discovered on farmland. It had been badly mauled and its injuries were consistent with it having been killed by a predator of the large-cat type. The following day a sheep was found dead on farmland in the Northchapel area nearby. The carcase had been almost completely devoured. Then, between 11 and 12 December, a sheep weighing 110lb was killed and eaten in a field, also in the Northchapel area. In the early hours of the morning of 13 December an 80lb ewe was killed and dragged almost 200yd before being partially eaten in the Lurgashall area. Its injuries were consistent with it having been attacked by a large cat-type predator.

More killings were reported at the beginning of 1965 and on the night of 17 January, an in-lamb ewe weighing about 150lb was killed on a farm in the Ewhurst area. Then, between 23 and 25 January a sheep was killed and almost completely eaten in a field on a farm at Northchapel. At about 5.15 in the evening of 27 January, a man reported seeing a large cat-like creature. He was driving along a road at Hurtwood when the animal crossed in front of him. Other people reported seeing large cat-like animals in the area of Hurtwood Common, and eventually ranger Ron Ware issued a public warning that it was believed a puma was wintering there in the woods, advising people, especially children on horseback, to be careful.

On 15 February a puma-like big cat was sighted at Holmbury St Mary. The cats then remained out of sight for a few weeks, or else people had given up reporting sightings. But from May until December, at roughly monthly intervals, puma-like animals were seen around Cranleigh and Chiddingfold. On 4 July a much more detailed report involved a number of people, including two members of the police force. The animal appeared to stroll across a meadow adjoining the home of the Queen's cousin, the Reverend Andrew Elphinstone, at Worplesdon near Guildford. At 11.40am Inspector Eric Bourn of the special constabulary, now retired, spotted the animal from his garden, only about 100yd away. A Post Office engineer working 20yd away shouted 'Look at that puma!' Inspector Bourn said:

I went to where he was standing and sure enough, without any doubt whatsoever, there was the puma. I watched it come out of the copse and walk along the side of the meadow, keeping to the cover of the hedge to within 100yd of the bottom of my garden. Then it lay down out of sight. It was a ginger-brown colour and the size of a Labrador dog. I rang the police. Just as they arrived it got up and sauntered back at a leisurely pace to the copse as I watched it through field glasses. I do not know whether it saw us watching but it was in no hurry as it went into Mr Elphinstone's copse and disappeared. We went over to where it had lain in the grass and found a half-eaten rabbit.

Motorcycle-patrol officer PC Robin Young — who has since left the force — had come in answer to the call to the police. He said:

The animal was in sight for about twenty minutes and there was no doubt that it was the puma. It was ginger-coloured and had a long tail with a white tip and a cat-like face. It was just walking casually round the meadow. I had a good look at it through binoculars from 60yd away. One of the villagers there had a shotgun and took a potshot. Then the animal took off. We followed it for about half a mile and then lost it when it reached the road.

Throughout the rest of the year there were many sightings of a puma-like animal. And at Witley on 13 September at about 11.30pm a dog was badly attacked. A large cat-like creature was suspected of causing the injuries.

On 22 September, about 7.15pm, a farmer noticed six of his cows grouped together in one of his fields at Whiteways Corner, Hog's Back. They were staring intently at another animal. The farmer approached to within 15–20yd of the puma-like creature which was playing about like a kitten. When it realised it was being watched, it bounded away in great leaps. This Hog's Back area was the scene of a number of sightings, including three by people driving along the Hog's Back itself. In one of these the driver swung his car towards the animal, in another the motorist and his companion stopped to look, so that visibility was good. All three described the creature as puma-like.

Reports for 1967 were few in comparison with those of former years. But in January, May, July and August, puma-like animals were seen in the Hog's Back, Hindhead, Pirbright and Chiddingfold areas. The August entry was the last recorded in the Surrey puma file of the Godalming police. Unfortunately the original files have now been destroyed and no actual statements taken from witnesses were kept. To illustrate how much information has been lost, we will return to Mr Edward Blanks, manager of Bushylease Farm at Crondall. Mr Blanks has now retired and in the early seventies the estate of Bushylease was broken up and sold, much of the area of woodland and scrub being dug up and destroyed. When I interviewed Mr Blanks, a very different story emerged from that in the police files of his having seen the Surrey puma over a number of years. He and his family had indeed had a number of sightings, but not of the same animal. Mr Blanks, in fact, remembers seeing large cat-like animals from approximately 1962 until 1971. Over this nine-year period he and his family saw at least three distinctly different animals, but only one was taken seriously by the authorities – the so-called puma, a large Great Dane-sized tawny creature with darker reddish-brown shading along its back. It was powerfully built with a long blunt-ended tail that curled at the tip. This animal appeared to show no aggression to humans, in fact it showed curiosity and the family was often conscious of being followed when moving around the farm at night. Sometimes a swiftly shone torch-beam would reveal a flash of glowing red eyes. Although it appeared to prey on both sheep and deer occasionally, its main diet seemed to be rabbits and even woodpigeons; indeed it was once seen to snatch a group of dead birds that the farmer had shot.

It made frequent trips into outbuildings and appeared to use straw as bedding some nights when it denned up there. It was associated with a very strong scent, by which the family learned to recognise when it was in the area. Cattle and dogs showed fear when in the presence of this odour, which was described variously as 'almost suffocating', 'musty, like rotting wood' and 'a strong smell with an ammonia tang'. This animal was accepted by the authorities, as it fitted their belief that a feral puma was living in the area. However, they did not accept a second animal that was seen a number of times, though less frequently than the tawny one. It was similar to the brown cat in size and build, but its coat was either dark grey or black. The third animal was more like the creature described so well by Mrs Arnold: it was smaller than the tawny and dark animals, and Mr Blanks saw it only three times. It was about the size of a medium dog like a spaniel, ginger-coloured with spots and stripes in a darker colour. It had a flat cat-like face with protruding fangs hanging over its lip. It was rather like a hybrid lynx as it had tufted ears but it had a long tail.

Although the Godalming police have closed their files on the puma, large cat-like animals are still seen in the area and reports trickle into the national press from time to time. In September 1980 reports of a sighting were received from the Guildford area. *The Sun* carried a report on 27 June 1981 that police were checking a trail that could have been made by a puma. However, the paper also adds that the Surrey puma had been reported but 'never seen in the 1960s'. It would be interesting to know if Ian Pert read the article. A former police photographer, he and a colleague took a photograph of a cat that was prowling around a field near his pub at Worplesdon. It had been seen by a number of people over a few days and Mr Pert took a photograph from a distance of about 35yd. Unfortunately the animal in the resulting picture could have been a feral domestic cat. But the disappointed photographer might take heart – Mrs Arnold, who gave such a splendid description of the cat she had seen on more than one occasion, stated that his picture was very like the animal she'd seen.

On 27 January 1970 Freda Siggers and a neighbour were walking their dogs in the early morning on Ash Ranges, near Aldershot, when the dogs started to show unease. As they started home there was a terrifying scream and a puma-like animal crossed the path about 20yd from them. In December 1970, cat-like prints were found in the snow in a garden at Farnborough.

The Odiham area produced a number of reported sightings throughout 1971 and 1972.

September 1972 produced a number of sightings at Fleet Station near Bushylease Farm. Dennis Long of Fleet saw the animal with a number of other witnesses. He said: 'We looked across the lines to the up platform and saw it behind the railings. It was very much like a big cat. It had a black head and a brown body with grey markings.' Railway worker Vic Carr confirmed the sighting. Adjoining the station car-park is Fleet pond. A reporter, Mr Deverell, went to the station to follow up the sightings, leaving his wife sitting in the car in the car-park. Suddenly she spotted a puma-like animal. She said: 'It went in and out between the cars carrying a fish in its mouth. It threw back its head and tossed the fish up, made a purring noise and caught it and went on out of sight.'

In March 1973 sweet-shop proprietor Charlie Christopher of Cove Road, Farnborough, was out cycling at 6 o'clock one morning. As he went up Frimley Bridges, during the day one of the busiest stretches of road in Britain, a large puma-like animal suddenly loped across the road in front of him. He told reporter Alan Franklin, 'Now I am a confirmed believer in the puma. The way it whipped across the dual carriageway, and then turned round and stared, really startled me.'

In June the same year a large cat-like animal was seen by two policemen in the Queen Elizabeth Park, Farnborough, at 4.20am from a distance of about 10yd. Police Constable Anthony Thomas, who had been eight years in the force, said, 'It was in the early hours of the morning but the light was good. It stood about 10yd away from me. It was three or four times the size of a cat, with a long tail and pointed ears. It was definitely not a dog or a fox. But I'm not saying it was definitely a puma.'

Encounters have also taken place over the years further into Hampshire. The first clearly recorded sighting was by Mr A. Burningham one early evening in late August 1959 when he was driving along a quiet country road near Godsfield Copse, south of Preston Candover and 5 miles north-east of Winchester.

Suddenly 'an enormous great cat' crossed the lane about 40yd ahead of him. It was about the same size as a Labrador dog but its features and gait were definitely feline rather than dog-like. It had a rather mangy-looking coat, pointed ears and a long tail that curled up at the end. As Mr Burningham stopped his car and watched, the animal appeared to be stalking lambs in a nearby field.

In October 1964, just about five years after Mr Burningham's sighting, a gamekeeper reported having shot at a 'black slit-eyed' panther-like animal at Farley Mount near Winchester. Police received reports of an injured puma but a search of the area produced nothing. However the publicity produced a statement from another gamekeeper at Kings Somborne, 7 miles west of the city. He reported seeing a similar animal on two occasions.

In February 1965, in the Winchester area, a gamekeeper Michael Lewis, accompanied by his brother David, discovered very large cat-like prints that could have been made by a puma-sized animal.

Mr and Mrs Harding of Selborne were also quite certain that the animal they saw in the early hours of 1 January 1976 was neither dog, fox nor feral domestic cat. They were driving in the Alton area, with Mrs Harding's parents, when suddenly they spotted a huge black panther-like cat. It crossed in front of the car from a side lane, causing Mr Harding to brake sharply. To their amazement, instead of making off the animal let its curiosity get the better of it and slowly walked up to look at the car. The four occupants watched as the animal walked around the car, sniffing at the wheels and doors, giving them an excellent opportunity to study it at close quarters. Mr Harding said: 'It was between the size of a red setter and a Great Dane, powerfully built, smooth-coated with a cat head and upright ears. Its colour appeared to be jet black.' Having fully investigated the car, the animal slowly walked away to disappear into the hedgerow. The family decided not to report the incident to the police because, as it was New Year's Eve, they felt that there would be no chance of anyone believing them – in fact Mr Harding felt that if he reported the sighting he would probably be booked for drunken driving, or at least accused of it.

Two more sightings of puma-like animals were reported to the police in 1979. One was at Hollycombe, near Haslemere, and the other was in a railway cutting at Liphook. Then on Sunday 14 March 1982, ambulance driver Mr Pickhaver was driving along the Haslemere road towards Linchmere at 11.30am. As he passed Marshes Hollow Lane he spotted a grey cat-like animal about 3ft 6in long, crouched in a stalking position in a field of sheep and horses. Mr Pickhaver said, 'I don't believe in this sort of thing. I don't believe in ghosts and I don't believe in pumas, I hadn't even read details of the other sightings when I saw it. The pubs weren't open at that time and I don't even drink.' He went home for his binoculars and later walked over the fields to try and identify what he had seen. He said, 'The sheep were quite different, this animal had a smooth close coat. I know a nearby house owner has a grey Great Dane, but it could not have been that, it would be much too tall and could not have got into the crouching position to stalk. The animal was definitely feline.' His colleagues at the ambulance station in Haslemere don't believe him, nor does anyone else. He says 'I know what I saw'. He reported his sighting to the police but they too were sceptical. The duty officer said, 'If there's an animal like that on the loose, why don't we find carcases of animals it has killed?' Obviously the duty officer had never read the day-book of his colleagues at Godalming police station.

The New Forest is also in the picture. On 4 February 1965, seventeen-year-old Felicity Whiteway was cycling near Ashurst where she lived, when suddenly a leopard-like animal leapt out of the bushes in front of her. The police found nothing, but gave out a public warning for people to take care in the area. There followed a number of sightings in the area throughout 1971 and 1972.

In February 1972 Mrs H. Short of Tatchbury Lane, Winsor, near Woodlands, discovered large cat-like prints in her garden, revealing claws 1½in long. The same year Mrs Cron found similar prints near her New Forest home, also showing claws. Her three sons, Stuart aged twelve, Andrew aged ten and Donald aged six, were playing at the edge of the New Forest when they spotted a strange animal creeping through the grass. Andrew got closest to it and described it as 'larger than an Alsatian dog but it looked like a cat. It had a big head with stick-up ears like a cat's ears and its eyes looked fierce.' At first the boys thought it was a tawny-brown colour. Frightened, Andrew slapped his dog's lead against his leg and the animal, startled, bounded off in great leaps. As the boys ran home, their Alsatian, frightened, ran with them, making no attempt to chase the cat. Later Andrew pointed out a photograph of a puma as like the animal they had seen. Throughout 1973 sightings continued to be reported in the New Forest.

Sussex seemed to take some of the overspill of animals from her neighbours. During the night of 23 November 1965, a sheep was killed and almost completely devoured on a farm at Plaistow. At Shillinglee on 9 August 1966 at 11.00am a man reported seeing a strange cat-like animal in a copse. He described it as a puma.

In March 1975 two girls were out horse riding at Horsham, West Sussex. When they were near Brooks Green, south-west of Horsham, a large cat-like animal bounded out in front of them, startling both mounts and riders as it crossed their path. Two days later a woman reported seeing a puma sitting by the roadside. This was on the other side of Horsham, along the M23 motorway at Pease Cottage.

The next recorded sighting occurred near Ashdown Forest. It was in the summer of 1980 when H. H. C. Weaver was walking through woods near Linfield. To quote his own words:

I was walking along a grassy woodland path with a friend when we both became aware that about twenty yards in front of us, walking in the same direction, was a large black cat. We could hardly believe what we saw as it was about 18 inches high and very definitely alien to anything one would expect to see of the feline species in this country. The features about the animal that made a great impact on

61

us were the shiny sleekness of the animal and it appeared to have a black bushy tail. We stopped our forward progress because it was so unexpected and a little 'scary'. Within seconds it veered off the path and disappeared down a bank covered with heavy undergrowth.

Mr Weaver's black cat is certainly in keeping with a number of other black puma and panther sightings. But the same can't be said for the sighting that Mrs Joan Gilbert reported on 7 April 1974 in Dorset. At 3.30am she saw a strange animal loping in a cat-like manner across Western Avenue at Branksome, between Bournemouth and Poole. She said, 'It had stripes, a long thin tail and seemed to be all grey though it might have had some yellow on it. It was thin and definitely not a fox.' Later she was shown some pictures of large cat-like animals, but she chose a very different creature. The nearest picture she could find that resembled the animal she had seen was that of a Tasmanian wolf. But Mrs Gilbert must have felt a great deal better to learn that two men had reported seeing a similar animal in 1972 and 1973, though their sightings were far away, in Kent. Mr Peter Cookson of Lympne was driving between Canterbury and Lympne at about 3.30am in June 1972 when a large cat-like animal bounded across the road. He too felt it looked like a Tasmanian wolf, because of its yellow-and-grey stripes. However he didn't report the sighting until January, after Mr Fred Arnold of Folkestone saw a large grey-and-yellow animal bound across the road in front of him as he drove from Capel to Alkham. A gamekeeper and RSPCA inspector Tony Jepsom examined puma-like tracks in the area.

Lorry driver David Black was even luckier in having his sighting verified by others. At 1.00am on 18 July 1963 he was driving on Shooters Hill, south-east London, when he saw what appeared to be an injured dog by the roadside. He stopped his lorry to check the animal. He said, 'I walked over to it and then it got up. I knew then it wasn't a dog. It had long legs and a long pointed tail that curled up. It looked as if it had a mouthful of food. It ran off into the woods.' A police patrol car checked this area of woods and common, and they spotted a cheetah-like animal that actually leapt over the bonnet of the car as they gave chase. Other people reported sightings. A search of the area revealed large cat-like tracks along a stream bed. They were larger than the prints of the tracker dogs and the claw indentations were clearly visible.

On 23 July Mr Jim Green, head groundsman of the nearby Kidbrooke Sports Club, reported hearing a 'loud snarling noise. It sounded like a fighting cat, only much louder'. At the nearby Royal Air Force base a security sergeant and a constable heard snarls and saw a big dark animal silhouetted against a cricket screen. However, a police search in the area again produced nothing.

As I live there at present, I have myself made an extensive study of Devon sightings. Dominating the county is the Dartmoor National Park, covering 365 square miles of moorland and granite hills. Scattered over the moor are woods and forestry plantations, and surrounding it is rich agricultural land, the fields ending in steep-sided wooded valleys. It is a remote, wild and beautiful countryside, a haven for holidaymakers in summer but a bleak and dangerous place in winter. It has large stretches of woodland containing ancient oaks, beech, chestnut, sycamore and silver birch. A number of the forests are Forestry Commission land consisting of mixed conifers, including spruce, fir and pine. It is the habitat of a wide variety of wildlife, certainly enough to support a sizable carnivore.

Most famous are the Dartmoor ponies, although it is not really correct to class these as wild, for all ponies grazing the moors are privately owned. However, they roam freely, being rounded up and sorted once a year in time for the annual horse sales, when the stallions are chosen and the youngsters are separated from the brood mares. Deer are well represented in the forests: fallow are the most common, but red and roe can be found in some areas and a newcomer on the scene is making itself noticed – the tiny Chinese muntjac deer. Foxes and badgers are common in the woods, as are squirrels and smaller rodents, whilst the grasslands support both hares and rabbits. That strange animals can breed there unnoticed is proved by the recent colonisation of woods near Okehampton by porcupines that escaped from a wildlife park. Despite the fact that they have been classified as an official pest by the Ministry of Agriculture, I have not met anyone who is certain where they are breeding or, to date, how their numbers have increased. As well as ponies, cattle and large flocks of sheep graze on the moors. One farmer recently remarked to me that he could lose fifty sheep a year and not even notice the loss; however, not all farmers feel the same way. The *Mid Devon Advertiser* published the following article in 1979:

> Dartmoor farmers who accept that they might lose ten per cent of the sheep they run on the moor annually are becoming alarmed at their increasing losses, which many are reluctant to put down to natural wastage.
> Mr Dick Perryman of Manaton has lost fifty ewes and lambs over the past year. He has advertised the loss in case some have strayed into other flocks but so far has had none returned and is not optimistic about getting them back.
> Mr Harold Wonnacott of Thornworthy, Chagford, who has had sheep on the moor for fifty years has lost sixteen since the middle of July. Mr Wonnacott continues, 'I've a neighbour who had about 140 sheep. He used to lose about twenty every year and when there were only twenty left he sold them and finished with it.'
> Mr Tom Pollard of Beestor, North Bovey, who has lost twenty sheep, said he would normally expect to lose four or five out of every hundred on the moor but would put that number down to natural wastage.

The article continued to discuss whether the losses resulted from sheep-rustling. Taking this area as just one tiny part of the whole of the moors, it gives some idea of the amount of stock that can be lost through natural causes or otherwise.

In June 1977 a story appeared in the local newspapers that made headlines in the nationals. RSPCA inspectors were called out to Lower White Tor on Dartmoor to investigate the finding of a number of animal carcases. There were reported to be fifteen dead ponies, a bullock and a sheep. Inspector Gordon said: 'They are so badly decomposed that we just do not know what

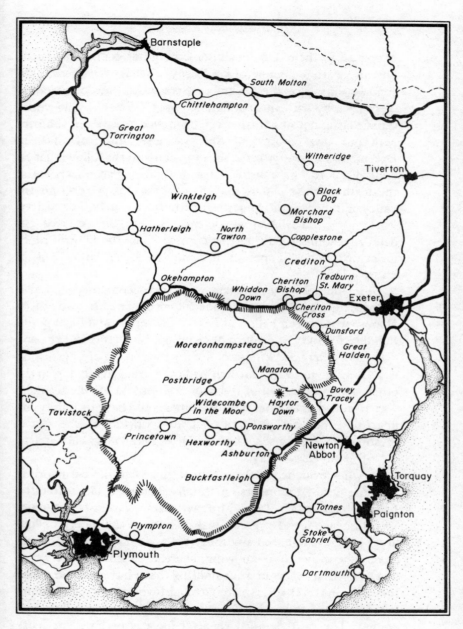

Map 3 Area of Devon sightings

65

Eyewitness Accounts

happened to them. Obviously something has gone on up there, but no vet that I know of could say what it was at all.' Mrs Joanna Vinson of the Dartmoor Livestock Protection Society wasn't happy with this verdict. She said: 'We are by no means satisfied that nothing further can be proved and we will continue with our own enquiries.' She obviously did just that. In December the same year the society published the following in its annual report: 'We consider there was violence connected with the deaths of these ponies, that their deaths took place within the valley and that they did not die from natural causes. The society, working with the Animal Defence Society, has carried out detailed examinations of the carcases and found broken or dislocated bones, apparent bruising on bones and signs of massive bleeding.'

Unfortunately, the carcases were too decomposed to tell if they had been eaten. Unlike one found by Theo Brown, FRAI Honorary Research Fellow at Exeter University and Recorder of Folklore for the Devonshire Association. She wrote in her book *Tales of a Dartmoor Village* of finding the carcase of a dead pony at Postbridge in 1950. One half had been dragged 50yd from the other, around the wall of the Scotch sheepfold. At the time she was mystified as to what type of animal could have torn the pony apart and then dragged half of it such a distance. She was as mystified as Mrs Vinson when the latter found large claw-marks on a tree at Hexworthy.

So what evidence is there that a large cat-like carnivore is roaming across the moors? After all many naturalists, like the badger champion Ruth Murray, deer wardens and conservationists, spend a great deal of time in the lonely upland areas but have not seen anything. Yet a great number of people have. The difficulty is knowing where to begin.

The earliest report of a cat sighting that I have read occurred sometime in the 1930s. An archaeologist working on a dig on the moor reported that whilst working he had seen a puma-type animal. The next detailed report I have is perhaps the most conclusive record of all the Devon sightings. In late summer

66

1963 Mr Richard Frost was out shooting rabbits with his brother-in-law, who now lives in New Zealand. They were near Whiteworks near Swincombe, not far from Hexworthy where Mrs Vinson some years later found the claw-marks. Suddenly they put up an animal about the size of a Labrador dog, and instinctively Mr Frost's brother-in-law shot it. Let Mr Frost tell his own story:

We'd been rabbiting and I was carrying a rabbit with my gun under my left arm so I couldn't use it. My brother-in-law was walking slightly ahead of me going back to the car which was left by the road at Whiteworks. It was true to say that we'd no right to be there whatsoever, but still my sheep did run up into that area when they were on the moors in the summer and the presence of such an animal was definitely, I felt, a threat. Now I don't know whether Stewart actually stepped on it but it seemed to get up, almost at his feet, from the heather round the rocks that line the path there, and he hesitated before he fired. I encouraged him to knock it over and he's a fairly good shot. He'd also got a rather more than usually powerful shotgun and he was able to bring it down and it was absolutely stone dead. He'd hit it at the back of the neck and the base of the skull. We looked at it and wondered what to do for a moment or two and I said, 'I'm very glad that that's not about if my ewes are up here'. He said, 'Well that must be true. I wonder if it's a protected animal, I think we'd better keep quiet about this,' which we accordingly agreed to do. We moved it on a bit to the edge of the clay pits where there was a good soft hole in which it could be readily and quickly interred, which is what we did, and we then went on with our rabbits and finished the evening.

Mr Frost then continues to describe the animal:

It was certainly much bigger than I expected. I thought at first that it was some weird sort of fox. It was hurrying and could easily have been a fox by its gait. It was evening time and the light was already failing and I don't think I took much note of the colour until I handled the dead pelt. It had what I would describe as a half tail and it was spotted over the quarters, the spots becoming more stripes as you went forward along its body. It had a face like a much bigger domestic cat but the one overriding feature was the large tufted ears. The ears were full of hair and there were tufts of hair on the back of each ear. There was quite definite coarse hair on the back of each ear. There were quite definite coarse whiskers. The underparts were yellow, but I wouldn't like to be any firmer than that. Certainly they were lighter than the body. At this time I couldn't be sure but I seem to remember a rather dark tail, complete. There might have been one or two bands as you got nearer to the animal's rump. The feet were noticeably very powerful. Whether the claws were in or out in life I couldn't say, but certainly after it had died the claws were evident. They were quite definitely evident after it was dead.

Unfortunately there is no chance of retrieving the bones of the animal after such a long period of time. Even if the carcase had not been dug up and carried away piecemeal, the soil of the moors has a quick-lime property, and bones rot and disintegrate within a couple of years. In another part of the country it would have been worthwhile excavating in the region of the clay pits, but not on Dartmoor.

The same year a number of reports were received from the Tiverton area, claiming sightings of a large puma-like animal. Mr Brick Francis of Paignton Zoo was called in and did indeed find cat-type tracks. However, on receiving information that someone in the area owned a Great Dane, he didn't make further reports. No one attempted to match the Dane prints to the pug-marks, or even to check if the dog had been roaming about when people saw the cats.

The next animal to be clearly seen was a very strange one, in June 1969. Colonel W. A. C. Haines of Brushford was driving near Witheridge, 10 miles west of Tiverton, scene of the 1963 sightings, when he spotted an animal by the roadside. He watched it in brilliant sunshine for about three minutes from a distance of 15ft.

I have seen many leopards in Malaya and it was exactly like one, but smaller although it was the size of a calf. At first I thought of a Great Dane or fox gone wrong but it was far bigger than a fox. I am nonplussed: I just do not know what it was.

It had a brown head, large black prominent eyes and a nose extraordinarily like a pug. Its left ear was pricked but the other hung down as if torn. Its ribs were a bright pale chestnut turning to a sort of dirty gingery-brown and its hindquarters were darker still. On its hindquarters were three black spots about the size of a penny and along its spine was a ridge of hair about two inches in length which waved in the breeze. Its body was smooth-haired and thin. Its tail, long and thin, looked like a piece of dirty rope. Its legs were very long for its body and pale fawn in colour.

This statement was made by Colonel Haines at the time of his sighting. When I questioned him, twelve years later, he was still convinced that he had seen a strange type of large cat. He had made his own enquiries and discovered that a number of sightings had occurred two years before in 1967. He had also traced other witnesses who had seen the same rather tatty and apparently elderly animal that he had seen in 1969, including a local blacksmith.

Theo Brown can remember hearing vaguely about pumas for several years in the 1950s and 1960s. In her report on Folklore in the *Transactions of the Devonshire Association* for 1971, which covers the year 1970, under the heading 'Black Panther', 'Puma', she wrote:

> Numerous reports appeared in the Press from April and all through the summer months of a cat-like monster seen in places very far apart – Tedburn St Mary, Dulverton, near Clovelly, Cheriton Bishop, Plympton, Haldon . . . Assuming that these two different-coloured creatures are anything more exotic than a stray deer from Haldon or a large ginger tom, there must be several at large. But no devastation of poultry, etc., has been reported.

One person who didn't need convincing that the cats existed was farmer John Anthony, whose farm lies between Tedburn St Mary and Whitestone, and who over a period of years often spotted a dog-sized black cat on his land. Across from his fields was a wooded hillside and he frequently saw the cat crossing the fields to and from the woods. Once, when he was out shooting foxes at night and using the distressed rabbit call, he swung his spotlight round and picked out the cat standing watching him, its eyes glowing red. Another time he spotted it within 30yd of his farmhouse. He estimated it to be about the size of an Alsatian dog, weighing about 70lb. It was jet black with a cat-like face and upright pricked ears. The long tail was blunt-ended like a leopard's. When it moved it did so very quickly with a cat-like bounding movement. Mr Anthony estimates that he saw the cat more than thirty times over the years. 'Why did you never report it?' I asked.

His answer was reassuringly simple. 'It wasn't doing me harm. Why should I bother it? If it had taken stock, then I would have shot it, but it didn't so I just let it be.' He also admitted he had grown quite fond of the beast. Eventually a new dual carriageway was built, dividing his land from the woods, and he no longer saw the animal.

Another gentleman who had a number of sightings was Police Sergeant John Duckworth. He was a motor-patrol officer based at Tavistock, and whilst driving about the Devon roads at night he had a number of sightings of a large black cat-like animal. He kept records of his own sightings in the Whiddon Down area, at Tedburn St Mary and also at Tavistock, and took a personal interest in following up other people's sightings. Later he was transferred to Okehampton. Although I have spoken to colleagues, unfortunately Police Sergeant Duckworth died tragically so I was unable to obtain any details of his investigations.

I could however speak to another man who had multiple sightings, and although he too has seen large black dog-sized cats he certainly hasn't seen the same animals as John Anthony or Sergeant Duckworth. Mr Kingsley Newman has a 35 acre holding about 40 miles south of the other sightings, on the River Dart at Stoke Gabriel. Since the late 1970s he has been losing chickens. Blaming foxes, he waged war on poor old reynard; but no matter how many foxes he shot, he still lost stock. Finally, he erected a large walk-in trap and baited it. He certainly caught something, for the following day he found his trap a heap of twisted metal with the metal bolt bitten clean through. Mr Newman asked Jack Davey, Vertebrate Pest Adviser with the

Ministry of Agriculture, for advice. Mr Davey examined the trap. He said that some large or strong animal destroyed the trap but that there was no evidence to show what it was.

However, evidence was forthcoming. Since the destruction of the trap, Mr Kingsley Newman has five times seen large black panther-like cats on his land. One night when swinging into his driveway, he picked out not one, but two, animals in his car's headlights. He jumped out of his car and raced indoors for his gun, determined to finish the matter one way or the other. When he returned, one cat was still in sight drinking from a water-trough near his tractor shed. He fired the shotgun at the animal, peppering the wall with pellet, and the cat made off behind the shed. Without thinking Mr Kingsley Newman pursued it into the enclosed space between the shed's rear wall and the incompleted extension wall adjoining his field. He swung his torch round, finding nothing. Then in horror, realising how foolhardy he had been in the heat of the moment, he swung his light-beam upwards. Crouched on a beam overhead was the cat, its eyes blazing red in the torchlight. He described it as larger than a springer-spaniel dog with a cat-like face and furry ears. It had a low tail that swung down, lashing in front of him. He described the tail as being blunt-ended like a leopard's, not tapered like a domestic cat's. Its coat was thick and blue-black, 'almost the colour of burning tyres'. Mr Kingsley Newman had made a mistake, but to the cat's credit it wasn't a fatal one: instead of springing on to its attacker, the cat snarled and then leapt over the far wall and out of sight into the nearby field.

The following morning, having recovered somewhat from his shock. Mr Kingsley Newman examined the soft mud around the water-trough. He found distinct pug-marks and was able to take an excellent cast. Mr Davey returned to look at the paw-prints but could make no suggestion as to what had made them, so Mr Kingsley Newman, armed with the casts, went to nearby Paignton Zoo. There he saw Mr Brick Francis, the same Mr Francis who nearly twenty years earlier had been called in on the Tiverton sightings. He agreed that Mr Kingsley Newman's casts did look suspiciously cat-like. And Mr Kingsley Newman continued to lose his chickens. I myself tracked the animal a number of times across his land and scented it nearby, but I was unable to determine in which woods the animal was denning up. I did however find evidence of a cub the following spring and was able to take casts of the pug-marks.

A doctor driving through Stoke Gabriel one night also saw a large black puma-like cat, although he only reported his sighting to an ambulance driver in the area. Mr Mike Bronstow of Paignton also caught sight of a large cat-like animal at Stoke Gabriel. He owns an Irish wolfhound which he exercises through the woods every day. In the late spring of 1981 he was walking past the old quarry near Well Farm when he saw a large reddish-brown cat-like creature leap over a wall. What interested him most was the movement. Although he did not get a good look at the head, he said: 'It was cat-like because of its sinuous and fluid movement as it almost wriggled away through the rocks. It was about the size of a red-setter dog.' As he owns a red setter as well as a wolfhound he is familiar with the movements of large dogs.

Mr Bronstow wasn't the only person to see a large brown cat. Around 1978 to 1979 a number of people reported a golden or reddish-brown puma or lion in the Moretonhampstead area. The main scare began when a young couple on holiday who had been walking in the neighbouring woods contacted the police declaring they had seen a lion. They stated that they had seen a man with a lion and an Alsatian dog. The two animals appeared to be playing when the lion turned nasty. The man called the dog, jumped in his car and drove off, leaving the lion behind. The story had a mixed reception. One interviewing policeman was convinced that the couple were lying, yet they appeared to be genuinely upset by their experience. However, no one else in the area had seen either the car or the man with the animals. And surely no one could drive far with a car containing a lion without being noticed? Certainly not in a small town like Moretonhampstead, where even in the holiday season holidaymakers are noticed and remarked upon. Still, the police and wardens did mount a search but found nothing.

Yet people did see the so-called lion. And in 1970, people had reported puma-like cats at Cheriton Bishop just a short distance away. Sightings of the animal continued, but if it was the same animal as had been seen in 1970, why did the couple tell the involved story about the man and his dog? Unfortunately they left without giving any more information and, being holidaymakers, they are impossible to trace. However their story could have been true, or, at worst, part-true. One possibility is that they really did see a man exercising his dog, and that the cat was disturbed by the Alsatian – that the animals were never together or playing. In fact the probably terrified man was frantically calling his dog to safety, and that was why he leapt into the car and drove away. If so, why didn't he report his experience to the police? Possibly because he didn't think anyone would believe him – or else he didn't want to get involved. Another theory is that the man was exercising a lion and a dog, and the lion got out of hand and he abandoned it, just as the couple said. But again it is unlikely that such an animal could be transported any distance without someone noticing it. And if it was tame enough to carry in a car, it it doubtful that he would drive off and leave it. After all abandoning a lion isn't quite like abandoning a dog.

A third possibility is that the young couple really did see a large wild lion or puma-like cat in the woods – their terror seemed genuine – and wondered how they could get people to believe them. They would have no idea that others had also seen such animals over the years. If they invented the story of a man and his dog, that would account for the lion being there, and would give a reason for the police to mount a search. Unless the couple one day come forward and tell the full story, we shall never know what really happened that day in the woods near Moretonhampstead. We do know however that sightings of a tawny or brown cat continued.

One witness saw a Labrador-sized sandy-coloured puma-like cat that loped across the road at 8 o'clock in the evening during the summer of 1977. He said it was definitely not a dog. 'I'm convinced in my own mind that it was a cat. I was driving along the road from Bovey Tracey towards Haytor Vale when the animal ran across the road in front of me. Its movements were completely feline, not at all like a dog.' Haytor is only a short distance from Moretonhampstead. Yet another witness to a sandy-coloured large cat in the area was an off-duty policeman. Police Constable Farquharson was out hunting with the Mid-Devon Hunt when the hounds caused a golden Labrador-sized puma-like cat to break cover. The dogs set off after the animal but were recalled by the hunt master. On expressing his surprise at seeing the animal, PC Farquharson was told that such sightings were well known in the area. This occurred in February 1980.

The people of Moretonhampstead were not alone in having unusual feline neighbours about this time. Tedburn St Mary, between Okehampton and Exeter, had as already mentioned produced sightings for years. Not only locals were privileged to meet the Tedburn St Mary black panthers. Mrs Alice Moule of Shropshire, on holiday in the area, on 17 September 1980 was driving with her family from Cheriton Bishop towards Tedburn St Mary when they suddenly spotted a huge black cat. She said: 'We actually saw what I afterwards described to everyone as the biggest black cat I had ever seen! It was stalking along a row of bushes towards a ditch from a wooded area.'

The following year the black cats really made themselves noticed. In late January 1981 young Ben Huggins and his friend Peter Tremere were playing in the woods near Ben's father's Spicery Farm. They had a large tyre hanging from a tree to use as a swing and they certainly weren't expecting to see anything larger than a fox or rabbit. The two Jack Russell dogs suddenly went speeding off into the trees and the boys presumed they had gone after a rabbit. They weren't prepared for what followed. Suddenly the dogs came racing back yelping in terror, hotly pursued by a large black leopard-like cat. On spotting the boys, the cat stopped, paused for a moment, then turned and bounded up the wooded bank out of sight. Recovering from their fright, the boys decided to say nothing, convinced that the adult world wouldn't believe them. However a friend of Ben's father, Tedburn man John Bastin, mentioned having seen huge tracks in the woods and the story came out. Casts were made of the prints, the RSPCA were called in and the police alerted. The tracks were identified as being of puma type, and the officials believed they were dealing with an escaped or abandoned pet that had adapted to living in the wild. Inspector Roach of the RSPCA said, 'If it was a puma that was seen in woods near Spicery Farm, Tedburn, it would be extremely difficult to find. It would most probably shy away from human beings. It would certainly see us coming before we saw it.'

However, although it might have avoided the RSPCA it certainly didn't remain hidden. A few days later a worker felling trees saw a cat crossing a field towards Oldridge Woods. But the puma-sized black cat appeared to have acquired company, for a small black animal seemed to be trailing behind. Ben and Peter were now fully involved with puma-spotting and they told a similar story. Whilst playing a few days later in the trees near the Lily Brook, they once again spotted the cat. This time it was crouched down drinking from the stream, and sitting beside the big cat was what the boys described as a 'tiny black puppy-like animal'. It would appear that the Tedburn St Mary cat had become a mother. I myself, together with a reporter from Devonair radio station, found tracks in this area the same week. On the bank of the stream, leading to the water's edge, were large cat-like prints, closely followed by tiny paw-prints the size of a domestic cat's. The small prints trailed so closely behind the larger animal's that they were superimposed where the small animal had trodden into the prints of the large. And yet the bank was broad enough for a number of animals to move side by side.

A lorry driver from Crediton, Mick Hallett, had also spotted the large black cat when driving along the dual carriageway just outside Tedburn. This is the same stretch of road that now divides farmer John Anthony's land from the woods where he used to see a large black cat. Mr Hallett saw the large leopard-like cat on two consecutive early mornings, running along the same stretch of road at about 3.30am.

The next spate of sightings occurred in the summer. In June, John Bastin was helping Michael Huggins with a barn roof when his son yelled 'Look at the cat!' Everyone on the ground turned in time to see a glimpse of a large black animal disappearing into some scrub and bushes.

Not far away from Spicery Farm, between Oldridge Wood and Whitestone Wood, Exeter University student Iain McWhirter was driving along the lane towards Copperwalls Farm where he was staying when, to his amazement, a huge black cat sprang down the bank into the roadway in front of his car. He braked and watched the animal as it paused then leapt up the bank and vanished over the hedge towards Whitestone Wood. A road-worker further up the lane had also watched the animal, but seemed totally unconcerned by the whole incident. When Mr McWhirter spoke to him, the man just shrugged and explained it was just the Tedburn puma they had seen and lots of people roundabout were used to seeing it. Mr McWhirter described the animal as being the size of an Alsatian dog and jet-black in colour with a cat-like head and a long tail that curled slightly at the end.

In the same month, police and firemen were called out to a barn fire near Tedburn St Mary. While there they all witnessed a large sleek black puma-like animal drinking from a nearby stream. Police Constable Norris of Exeter jumped into his car to give chase to the animal, but it bounded off and disappeared into the trees. PC Norris said, 'There was no doubt in anyone's mind that it was the so-called Tedburn puma. It was leopard-sized and definitely a cat.' Just up the road from Whitestone Wood, towards Crediton, there were two sightings of a large puma-sized cat near Rudge Farm. But these cats were more like the Moretonhampstead animals than the Tedburn St Mary ones. Miss Lesley Bryant of Rudge Farm was one witness. In the spring she was driving down the farm lane. In her own words:

I was driving home at ten o'clock at night. I think it was the early part of spring 1981, when it's lambing and there were no leaves. I was up to Cleave and I drove out of our new lane and we've got a milk stand, a concrete one, where we stick our rubbish-bags and this thing was standing up with its front legs on it, and I thought obviously it was a very big dog. It was the same colour as a fawn Great Dane, maybe slightly darker. But it was much too long for a Great Dane, and then I drove the car towards it and it ran off and I got a back view. It went very fast. It had a blunt-ended tail and sort of cat ears but not pointed. It just turned in that old lane and jumped a five-bar gate with no trouble and disappeared. It was like a racy sort of lioness. It had a short coat and looked in good condition. It went across our field towards the wood.

A couple of weeks before, Miss Bryant had had another sighting of a large tawny Great Dane-sized animal, but that had been at a distance across the fields, near the same woods. She wasn't alone in seeing the Crediton lion. A vet, Mr Sylvester, driving along the same stretch of road towards Rudge Farm, had also seen it.

A different kind of 'sighting' took place nearby at Venny Tedburn, where Mr Vigers owned 75 acres including a wooded area where some large cat-like prints were seen. Although Mr Vigers himself hasn't to date seen a cat on his land, he has both heard and smelt something unusual. In 1981, he was walking through his wooded area when 'I came down across a damp place when I saw these prints ever so plain. I mean if I'd had any idea of taking anything from them, that was the place to do it because it seemed fresh. But in 30 acres of firs that you don't walk through it would be very difficult to find that exact spot again. But I did smell and I told my workmen when I come back, I said, "I must be daft", I said, but right over in the middle of the cover it seemed as if somebody was burning brussels sprouts. It was a sort of peculiar smell, as if someone had let brussels sprouts boil over.' A vet, Mr Pugsley, regularly went shooting on Mr Vigers' land and the adjoining wood. Although unlike his colleague Mr Sylvester he hadn't seen any cat, he did describe a terrifically strong 'tom cat' smell in the area, and believed it was possibly a scent left by an escaped puma that was living wild in the forested parts.

Mr Vigers wasn't finished though. He had arranged for some workmen to cut back some branches in the fir plantation and one evening he decided to take a handsaw and cut back some of the tangle. He said:

> I took the handsaw with me and I worked up through until it was nearly dark. And I thought, well I can't see what I'm doing very well now, I'll leave it. I came down across. There's a hill this side where the firs are and then there's a piece of open rather large coppice 15–18 acres, the opposite side. And I heard this deep growling, I would estimate it was about a gunshot or a gunshot and a half away from where I was. And then within a few minutes there was another different sound altogether, a different sort of growl, about two or three gunshots in the other direction towards the forestry land. And there was this other one that I heard first, sort of answered back. And the other one made a noise. I thought 'Well this is interesting,' so I thought, 'Well if I walk up across I'm bound to see something,' but it was getting dark. I walked up to a wet place where the two tracks joined but I couldn't see any tracks and I listened very carefully until it was really dark but I didn't hear any more.

In autumn 1981 the Tedburn St Mary cat began to make its presence known again. Young Ben Huggins needn't have worried about his parents believing him: his mother, Mrs Pauline Huggins, together with a friend, watched a large black cat cross a field below their bungalow. She couldn't give a clear indication of size, but she noted that the animal was enormous compared to a crow in the same field.

John Bastin's fourteen-year-old son Mark also had a close encounter with a huge black cat the size of a large dog. He was walking his whippet towards his grandparents' farm near Hackworthy Brakes across the dual carriageway from Tedburn St Mary, when the dog stiffened and started to growl. He looked up to see a huge black cat walking along the ranch-type fencing towards him. Mark stared at the animal, shocked, despite having glimpsed a cat previously at Spicery Farm and knowing that a number of his friends had seen such an animal – it was still large enough to frighten him. When he told his grandparents, it was learnt that his aunt, Mrs Shirley Wilson, had seen the cat a few days before in the same area but had been afraid to mention it for fear of being laughed at. Hackworthy Brakes is quite a distance from the main area of the Tedburn sightings, but is very close to the woods where farmer John Anthony frequently saw a cat before the new road divided his land.

In February 1982, a teacher from the Tedburn St Mary junior school suddenly met the animal he hadn't really believed his pupils had been seeing. Peter Rolf said:

On 31 January I was driving back from Bristol. It was about 3.00am, and I was heading towards Heath Cross. I came up through Whitestone on the old A30 road. Just before the farm on the left-hand side, about opposite Whitestone House, I suppose, I made a sighting of a rather unusual animal that I couldn't positively identify. I was unlucky enough to see only the back half of it, and it was unlike anything I'd seen before, judging by size, judging by the way it moved. The nearest thing I could describe would be a cat, in that its gait was swaying and it was in no hurry to move. I picked it out in my headlights and I was going at a fair speed so I managed to see the back-end and the tail more than anything. The back legs looked very powerful, and the tail itself I would describe as kind of tubular, perhaps about 1½in thick. The fur itself was black, perhaps a little bit charcoal grey at the ends, and the end part, the hairs from the last 4 or 5in of tail, appeared to come out at a different and wider angle to perhaps make a kind of tuft. The tail itself was sort of an upturned loop, dragging partly near the ground and pointing upwards towards the end. Judging from the rear end, I would estimate it to be about the size of a springer spaniel.

Mr Rolf was extremely excited about what he saw, and when he met young Ben Huggins at school they compared notes. But Ben, and he was a farmer's son, described his cat as bigger than a sheep.

A few miles away, at Tiverton, Mrs Jean Bishop was worrying about the huge black puma-like cat that she had seen on a number of occasions in or near her garden. Her home is the dower house of a nearby estate and so she is surrounded by forest land. Although in 1981, like Mr Kingsley Newman, she tried to get help, unfortunately she received very little worthwhile advice. A so-called expert from a wildlife park and a companion traipsed through the woods, shotguns in hand, and then informed her that it was probably a leopard and therefore very dangerous, so she should not walk under any trees. The RSPCA put a small trap in a tree and then, leaving the poor lady terrified, off they went. It cannot, indeed, be very comforting to live in the middle of a forest and be told never to walk under trees for fear that a man-eating leopard might drop down on your shoulders!

In 1970, across the border in Cornwall, cat sightings were reported in the Launceston area. Then, in about June 1973, Camborne man Mr Dave Nicholas was walking through Tehidy woods between Redruth and Camborne with a companion when they suddenly saw a large tawny cat-like animal walking slowly up the path ahead of them. Mr Nicholas said, 'It was a puma-coloured large cat which was heading in a northerly direction towards the coast. It was in the afternoon, if I remember correctly. It made no noise that I noticed and it did see us. The whole encounter lasted not more than a couple of minutes as we did not pursue the animal any further.' Not surprisingly they were a little frightened and returned back home the way they had come. They didn't report the incident because they did not think anyone would take them seriously.

From 1975 to 1977 I owned a smallholding at Pendarves, near Camborne, not far from where Mr Nicholas had his sighting. There was a large wooded estate nearby. In the spring of 1975 a large hut containing chickens was broken into, via a high window from which the wire mesh had been torn away. About six chickens had been taken. A few weeks later a full-grown male goat was tethered near three nannies, when it was attacked and killed. The body was half-eaten, but unfortunately I didn't see it. The other three goats, just a few yards away and tethered, were untouched. This did not seem consistent with an attack by dogs, and neither packs nor single dogs were observed near the scene, either before the attack or in the weeks that followed. In the autumn of 1976 the body of a half-grown billy goat was dug up from its grave and carried away, about four weeks after its death from natural causes. The ground was only excavated in the region of the grave, and the packing case that the animal was buried in had been torn open but still remained in the hole. There was no sign of drag-marks, and the only part of the body to be found after a thorough search was the broken tip of a horn where it had struck a stone as the carcase was being carried away. In the nearby St Day area, a large black Labrador-sized animal was reported to be killing sheep. And in the autumn of 1980 Mr Berry of Penhalvean spotted a large black panther-like animal standing near the entrance to Stithians Reservoir.

Wales

Wales, like Britain's other Celtic areas, Scotland and Cornwall, has its own population of large cats. In the 1950s Peter Callerton was out shooting rabbits in woods at Penllergaer, South Wales, when he suddenly saw a large grey cat. He said:

> I happened to walk around a corner and I came face to face with a cat which was about three or four yards from me. I was quite astonished to see it. It was about the size of a spaniel. I could quite easily have shot it but it just didn't enter my head to do so. I just wanted to look at it and, within a couple of seconds, bang, it was into the undergrowth and gone. It was a stripy colour with tabby-like markings basically greyish. It didn't have the brown markings of a tabby cat, it had greyish-type striped markings.

Mr. Callerton didn't report his sighting until many years later as, although interested in the animal, he felt he must have seen either a freak or an escapee from a zoo.

Another witness who at first kept silent was Mr Lewis Coles of Ynyston, Leckwirth, near Cardiff. In May 1977 he first saw what looked like a large cat, on his farmland. He said, 'It came out of a crop of silage I was cutting and ran for cover. It was about the size of an Alsatian and was light brown in colour.' Mr Coles did not report this at the time, but reports came in later of other sightings in nearby Leckwith Woods, which adjoin Mr Coles' 200 acre farm. In July Mr Coles said, 'I did nothing then, as it has not done any damage, but in the last few nights lots of people have heard a terrible screaming noise. I have told the police and Barry Zoo have been helping us look for it.' Mr George Palmer, co-owner of the zoo, spent four nights hunting the animal. He said, 'We have heard a sound like a puma or an ocelot or cheetah, although we have not seen anything. Nor can I find any tracks.'

The following year forester Bob Pearce was working in Margam Forest near Swansea when he spotted a large cat loping across a clearing. It was marked with spots and stripes and Mr Pearce was convinced that he had seen a lynx. A few miles away, in 1979, a group of men were working in an area of mine waste, reclaiming coal, when they spotted a large fox-coloured dog-sized animal with a cat's head. The creature bolted down one of the many mine-workings in the area. The men sent in two dogs to flush it out: one dog never returned, the second was so badly injured that it had to be destroyed. The large reddish-brown cat was left alone.

Mid-Wales next hit the headlines with cat sightings. In October 1980, just two weeks after residents across the border in the Wolverhampton area reported sightings of a black panther on the loose, farmer Michael Nash of Pontdrain Farm at Llangurig was puzzling over the carcases of four sheep. The animals had been eaten, with the fleeces peeled away from the bodies. Another animal was found still alive but with a large chunk of flesh bitten from its hindquarters. As Mr Nash explained, the dead animals appeared 'to have been turned inside out'. It was then noted that strange sounds like 'a drunken man snoring' had been heard at various times over the past month coming from a nearby hay-barn. A woman reported seeing a large cat-like animal on the nearby hillside, and other sheep carcases were found in the surrounding area. The hunt was really on when large 4in cat-like prints were found in the mud outside the barn. The alarm was given and, as RSPCA inspector

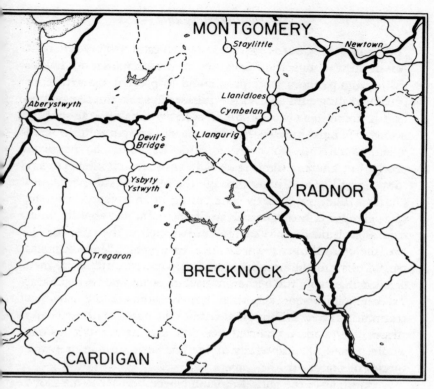

Map 4 Area of mid-Wales sightings

Trevor Caldwell put it, the circus began. On 24 October, police marksmen surrounded the barn with weapons powerful enough to stop a car, let alone a cat. Searchlights lit up the scene and even helicopters hovered overhead. However, alerted and careful, the cat must have slipped away before the full might of the law surrounded it, for the following day Alsatian police dog, Max, obviously showing more courage than sense, was sent burrowing into the bales of hay and straw. Happily for Max he found nothing, and lived to burrow another day. Police and RSPCA officials including Trevor Caldwell made a thorough search of the barn and found what appeared to be a denning-up area where the straw stank, as Sergeant Ken Davies said, 'like a big cats' house in a zoo'.

Although they were convinced that a big cat had been there, it was decided to suggest other causes for the animal sounds heard, to stop the panic of local people and to prevent the arrival of cowboys toting guns all over the hillsides. A spokesman suggested that it 'could have been a pair of barn owls making the snoring noises'. He must have crossed his fingers and spat into the wind when he said it! However, as often happens, the publicity brought in another sighting. A lady wrote from Chester to say that she had been driving through the Marteg Bridge area, not far from Llangurig, in the late spring of that year, when she spotted a puma lying sunning itself on rocks, just about 3 miles from Pontdrain Farm. Leaving her two girls in the safety of the car, she crossed over towards the animal, which leaped up and moved off into the bracken. She followed it a little way, then decided that to go further might be dangerous and turned back. To her amazement she then spotted another big cat that resembled a lynx, slightly smaller than the puma, with spots and stripes. She hadn't reported her sightings as she felt no one would believe her, especially as she had seen not one, but two, species of big cat in the same area.

A month after the barn drama, in November, Mr Ernie Lloyd of Coed Cae, Cwmbelan, saw a large puma-like animal only about 6 miles from Mr Nash's barn. He spotted the animal when he noticed his dogs and sheep defensively flocking together. A Mr Jones went to get some binoculars from a neighbour but the animal had disappeared, although tracks were found. Mr Jones said, 'The animal was a dark colour with some white on it. It was difficult to see what part was white because it was moving. It was the size of a large dog. The animal moved very quickly and ran in leaps and bounds like a cheetah. It looked as if it was scared and stopped from time to time and looked round. I haven't got any idea what it was, but it was definitely not a dog.' Mr Lloyd said: 'The tracks left by the animal were the size of a small palm with claws about the size of a finger. Police took casts of the prints.' Again, the report of one sighting produced others from different areas. At Church Stoke on the border between Powys and Salop, a large cat-like animal was spotted by a health visitor; and across the county at Staylittle near Llanidloes, a Powys County Council surveyor sighted a tawny-coloured puma-like animal.

The next sighting involving police activity was on 11 May 1981. The Dyfed-Powys police were called to Ysbyty Ystwyth, near Tregaron, where a large cat-like animal was reported to have killed seven ewes and five lambs. Again Trevor Caldwell was called in to assist. He said: 'The animal is almost certainly a panther. We have had three definite sightings in the last week from very level-headed people. It was described as a long jet-black cat, standing about 2ft 6in at its head. The countryside, with old mine shafts and quarries, is ideal for a big cat. Inspector Blyth and myself spent all day Wednesday looking for the animal, covering about 6 square miles. We found a number of paw-prints made by a large cat, especially by a small stream where it had been drinking.'

Back in Leckwith Woods, near Cardiff, South Wales, people were still seeing large puma-like animals. On Wednesday 10 June 1981, Mr Peter Coburn (who lives with Mr Cecil Bevan, Principal of University College, and Mrs Bevan) was driving home in the rain at 11.00pm when he caught sight of a lion-like animal in the light of his car headlights, sitting on the lawn in front of the Bevan's house, which is set back in 13 acres. Mr Coburn had seen the animal twice before in the drive leading to the house. Four months before he had seen the back and tail of the animal, and three months before he had spotted it standing in the same area. He said, 'It was about 3ft tall and a browny-tan colour. I am sure it is scared of people because it always makes a quick exit.'

In November 1981 Mr and Mrs Maggs of Tonmawr, near Neath, were driving through the village when a huge grey-and-black striped cat suddenly crossed the road in front of their Range Rover. It paused, and turned to look at them. Mrs Anne Maggs said, 'It was about 6ft long and about 2½ft high with really ugly features with a rather bulldog-like muzzle and striped and spotted markings.' The animal disappeared into the undergrowth of the hillside. Mr and Mrs Maggs were both shaken and curious but despite frantic searches through pictures of existing big cats, they couldn't find anything to match the animal they had seen. The nearest was a clouded leopard. They learnt later that an old man in the village, now deceased, had often talked of seeing giant cats in the area of Tonmawr. The sequel to this sighting by Mr and Mrs Maggs — the very recent developments — belongs to the last chapter.

In March 1982 I went over the area of the mid-Wales sightings with Inspector Trevor Caldwell, interviewed many witnesses and gained more information. Mrs Jones, living in an isolated area, had frequently seen a large black puma-like animal crossing the field in front of her cottage, heading towards a stream. Her last sighting had been just a few days before I arrived. Like Miss Chisholm of Inverness-shire, Mrs Jones is living in cat country. In the nearby woods, a local schoolboy had surprised a large black panther that was sunning itself on a rock. Even more surprised was a local district nurse who, whilst driving, had spotted a panther-like black cat running alongside her car. She was so shocked that she was unable to work for a couple of days. Also shocked was a taxi-driver who reported seeing a tawny, lion-like animal near Aberystwyth. The district nurse and the taxi-driver had joined a very exclusive club whose hundreds of members throughout Britain have had close encounters of the cat kind!

2

Sifting the Evidence

Unless one is willing to accuse very many respectable people, including vets, doctors and police officers, of lying if not of total insanity, there appear to be a large number of big cats roaming the British countryside. But what type of cats are they? It is time to examine the pieces of the jigsaw carefully and try to fit the bits together.

Of existing big cats, two can be dismissed as non-starters – the tiger and the jaguar. These two cats are much heavier and larger than any seen by eyewitnesses. The jaguar, for instance, weighs upwards of 300lb, the tiger is even heavier. Most sightings estimate the British cats as weighing between 70 and 120lb, far short of the minimum for the largest of the big cats. The lion, too, is an impossibility. Despite the many 'lioness' reports there have been no maned animals seen and, on closer examination, the lionesses become much more like pumas.

Next on the list is the panther or leopard, and the behaviour and habitat of this animal are worth a close look. Most people believe that leopards are shy creatures, living in remote areas, avoiding contact with man. It is a comforting thought, but wrong; in fact, the reverse is generally the case. Nairobi, capital city of Kenya, frequently plays host to visiting leopards, once darkness has fallen. The animals prowl through the streets and gardens, the only evidence of the visits the following day being the loss of household pets and livestock such as goats and chickens, and tell-tale pug-marks where the ground is soft. They are not heard and are seldom seen, although sometimes they can be observed, because, like so many territorial animals they often follow the same route night after night, until the food supply runs out or they are scared off. According to Edward R. Ricciuti, one such animal nightly visited the garden of a house, leapt up to the carport roof and settled there quietly, monarch of all it surveyed.

And not only in Nairobi. Sightings are not rare in South Africa's capital, too, and in 1976 the police shot a leopard in the city centre. Like our own town fox, the leopard not only adapts to man, but even takes advantage of him. And climate-wise it can live virtually anywhere – on snowy mountain slopes, in burning deserts, in tropical forests, on savannah and even in temperate woods such as our own. This versatility makes the leopard the most adaptable and least imperilled of all the big cats.

It is small wonder that the experts feel confident that, in the unlikely event of leopards 'going feral' in our countryside, there is little to prevent them thriving. But I challenge the opinion that if this takes place they will be obvious to the surrounding populace. If they can pad happily and unseen through cities where they are endemic, how much easier to sneak at night through the British countryside. Nocturnal, and apparently often black, what animal could be harder to see? There is even a species of leopard that produces a high percentage of melanistic, or black, animals in Malaya. Many of the British sightings report seeing black animals.

The size of the animals seen in Britain is also right. A leopard weighs, on average, between 100 and 150lb, the heaviest on record being 200lb. And pound for pound, the leopard has greater agility and strength than any other cat. To avoid the problem of scavengers stealing its kill, it makes a habit of carrying its prey up into the high branches of trees. Sensible perhaps, but not particularly impressive, not until you take into account that the victim often weighs twice as much as the predator and that the leopard carries its prey by the head, using its powerful shoulder as a support to lug the animal 40 or 50ft up into its chosen tree. Having put the food on the table, so to speak, the leopard will return again and again to the same prey until all is consumed. It is also a fairly tidy eater. Before taking its victim up into the heights it guts it, rather as we do to a carcase before hanging it up in the butcher's shop. At least if leopards are roaming our green and pleasant land, no one will have the unpleasant experience of rotting guts spilling down on them from overhead when taking a Sunday afternoon stroll through the woods.

In common with most cats, a leopard can cover up to twelve miles in a single night, but only if prey is scarce. Two or three miles will suffice if game is plentiful. With numerous rabbits in the countryside and placid flocks of unsuspecting grazing sheep, there does not seem much need for a big cat to travel far afield, except possibly when snow is on the ground. Then it need only go as far as the nearest hen-run or wandering dog or cat. In Africa, favourite food supplies are domestic goats and chickens. In Britain, substitute sheep for goats and you have a happy leopard, if an unhappy farmer. (Records give another favourite meal – baboon. The similarity between man and monkey has never been a comforting comparison – not even for the baboon.)

Although chickens and goats make easier prey, if any of the big cats should turn maneater, the leopard would be the most capable of taking on the task with distinction. It has had a lot of experience at the job: a million years ago in South Africa, a leopard dragged a dead young ancestor of *homo sapiens* to its tree. The fossil skull of the unfortunate Australopithecine apeman tells its tragic story today by the fang-marks preserved in the bone. Perhaps the animal was a direct ancestor of the terrible leopard that terrorised Panar in northern India earlier this century, killing 400 unfortunate souls. Or perhaps the one at Rudraprayag, although its total was a mere 100 victims.

That the problem is not considered solely one of the past was revealed in the 1970s when the World Wildlife Fund sponsored a study by a German scientist, Dr Hubert Hendricks, to look into the reasons why a few cats turn maneater. However leopards are quite happy to forgo actual killing, as they are not averse to eating carrion. This makes the possibility of trapping a live specimen a little easier as the cat will go for dead bait; if of course our British big cat is indeed a leopard. Many of the facts fit –

size, appearance and the number of black animals reported. But there is one glaringly obvious ill-fitting piece to this jigsaw: some of the animals seen have been reddish-brown, tawny-coloured or grey, and there is a lack of spotted coats. The melanistic variety is only a colour variation of the normal animal, not a sub- or separate species. Therefore, although black leopards are possible, non-spotted, plain-coated ones are not only unusual but don't exist – at least not according to the records.

The next animal to examine closely is the puma or, as it is sometimes called, the mountain lion or cougar. Indeed a large number of people, even police witnesses, have identified the cats as pumas. Their lifestyle, like that of the leopard, is normally secretive; in fact many rangers and wardens of wildlife parks and reserves where the puma is known to live have never caught a glimpse of one. Colour ranges from reddish-brown to pale golden-fawn, but is seldom black: a black form is not impossible, but very rare. And another characteristic of the puma is that although capable of attacking and seriously wounding if not killing a man, it has a pretty good record for non-violence. In fact it seems to have an inbred curiosity about humans and, when accidentally encountered, has been known to stand staring unabashed for a few minutes before making off. This pattern of behaviour has been noticeable during a great many of the meetings between man and beast in the British countryside. Often the cat has even gone so far as to sit down in a relaxed manner to continue its study of the strange two-legged animal. So behaviour and even colouration seem to make the puma the favourite for the title of large British cat. But is it?

It will be remembered that, on 4 July 1965 a large number of people witnessed a large puma-like cat at Worplesdon in Surrey. Two of the witnesses were policemen PC Robin Young, and Inspector Eric Bourn of the Special Constabulary. The cat remained in sight for some twenty minutes and PC Young studied it through binoculars from a distance of 60yd. This was no few-second glimpse of a moving animal by one or two startled witnesses, this was a careful study of an animal by men used to examining and recording evidence. So did they see a puma?

Robin Young had said, 'The animal was in sight for about twenty minutes and there was no doubt that it was the puma. It was ginger-coloured and had a long tail with a white tip and a cat-like face.' Eric Bourn had described it as 'the size of a Labrador dog'. Shape, size and colour were right, and all witnesses agreed it was puma-like. But what about the tail? No puma has a white-tipped tail, no known puma anyway. It has a white mark around its muzzle, but the tail is always black-tipped. So did all those witnesses on that sunny day at Worplesdon see a puma? There was no mention of the very characteristic white face markings a puma would be likely to have; and could Robin Young have been mistaken about the tail? It seems unlikely that people studying the animal for so long could all have made such errors in description. And if they didn't all make the same errors, then it wasn't a puma, or a known puma, that dined in leisurely style on its rabbit that July day.

But what about all the other sightings, the hundreds of puma-type cats that have been reported: did any of them mention a black-tipped tail? Unfortunately most descriptions give only the ground-colour of the animal and from that alone it has been described as a puma or puma-like. So the evidence is conflicting. There appear to be no other records of white-tipped tails, but nor does anyone mention them as black-tipped.

What are we left with? A large number of black animals that could be escaped melanistic leopards, and an even larger number of puma-type animals with or without the correctly coloured tail-tips. Could all these animals, ranging a territory from Tongue in Sutherland to Redruth in Cornwall, be escaped zoo animals or abandoned pets? It hardly seems likely that so many would have been held in captivity, never mind be living in a state of freedom. After all, keeping a tame leopard or puma is not something the average household contemplates when obtaining a pet. And even if it were a possibility, where are the spotted leopards? For a leopard, if it could change its spots, is hardly likely to abandon them completely. For the escaped-pet theory to be valid, a large number of traditionally coated big cats should have found their way into the woods and moorlands of our countryside. If they have, they are a great deal shyer than their black cousins, for reports of spotted cats are sparse indeed.

But not completely lacking. To quote again the description of the large cat seen by Christabel Arnold in the heart of the so-called 'Surrey puma' country:

> It had marks like a cheetah on its face and was greyish, browny-beige with spots and stripes. Its back was deep red-brown and massive at the back legs, which were striped black and red-brown right down. It had a white, beige and grey front ... it had a beautiful striped red-brown and beigy white-tipped tail. The stripes were as on the back legs with black thin lines. It had yellow slanted eyes, wire-like whiskers and tufted ears.

So what did she see? The tufted ears give a clue that it might have been a lynx. But such a theory is destroyed by the tail: not only that it is white-tipped, but that it is there at all. Members of the lynx family do range in colour from reddish-brown through to ginger and even grey. They do show a mixture of spots that run into stripes and they certainly do have tufted ears. But they don't have tails, at least not full tails. The lynx has a short bobbed tail. Indeed one member of the family is called the bobcat. So was Mrs Arnold mistaken about the 'beautiful tail'?

Mrs Arnold saw the animal on Bushylease Farm where Mr Edward Blanks was manager. That he and his family had a number of large-cat sightings on this land over a number of years has already been mentioned. Did he ever see the same animal as Mrs Arnold? He saw a cat the size of a spaniel dog, ginger with spots and stripes in a darker colour. It had a flat cat-like face with protruding fangs hanging over its lip, and tufted ears. And it had a long tail. But he and his family also saw a much larger puma-like animal, although they didn't notice whether it had a white-tipped or black-tipped tail. They also saw a dark leopard-like animal!

It's highly unlikely but just possible that Bushylease Farm played host to a selection of large feral cats: a puma, a leopard and a lynx; although even this selection does not account for that 'beautiful tail'. But could such an improbable combination of characteristics occur elsewhere? I thought again of Mr Richard Frost out shooting rabbits with his brother-in-law on Dartmoor in Devon, and of the fox-like animal his brother-in-law shot, fearing for the safety of the sheep that grazed nearby. When they examined the body they found they had killed a cat the size of a Labrador dog. Mr Frost had said:

> It had what I would describe as a half tail and it was spotted over the quarters, the spots becoming more stripes as you went forward along its body. It had a face like a much bigger domestic cat but the one overriding feature was the large tufted ears. The ears were full of hair and there were tufts of hair on the back of each ear.

Success in identification? Tufted ears and a short tail – a lynx? However when I showed Mr Frost a photograph of a lynx, he shook his head at the short bobbed tail: no, he hadn't meant that short. But what had he meant? He then described a tail of reasonable length but with a blunt end rather than a tapered tip. A tail in fact that one would expect to find attached to the rear of a juvenile leopard.

And what can one deduce from the already quoted sighting by Colonel W. A. C. Haines of a strange animal by the roadside near Witheridge, which he watched for about three minutes at close quarters? Colonel Haines described it as leopard-like, with a brown head, large black eyes and pug-like nose. Its pale chestnut ribs shaded to a dirty gingery-brown and its hindquarters, on which were three black spots about the size of a penny, were darker still. Significantly, the colonel said that along its spine was a ridge of hair about 2in in length though its body was smooth-haired and thin. Its long thin tail looked like a piece of dirty rope and its legs, very long for its body, were pale fawn.

Although Colonel Haines was alone when he saw this rather strange creature, a number of people reported that they too had observed an animal of the same or similar appearance. All agreed that they had not seen a dog of any kind, but no one could suggest a cat that looked just like this rather odd creature. It certainly was of the size and ground-colour of most of the 'pumas' seen, but the adult puma does not have black spots. Young cubs have spots along their backs, but these are lost as they grow older. And Colonel Haines's cat seems likely to have been a very old cat, judging by its thin and tatty appearance, or an ill one. And a new factor arises – the ridge of hair along the back. Other people saw it, but no one could explain it. The only known large cat with a crest or ridge of fur along its back is the cheetah. But cheetahs are most definitely spotted, never striped or black or gingery brown. And their spots do not consist of three penny-sized spots on their hindquarters.

This question of colour and size is complicated. For the last fifty years people have been seeing large cats in the forests and woodlands of Devon. And they still are. Some, like Colonel Haines, see gingery-brown animals, others report reddish-brown; but many more see black leopards or panthers. Like Mr Kingsley Newman, of Stoke Gabriel, whose cats are leopard-sized black animals. He said, 'They were the size of a medium-sized dog, long-bodied with rather a low-slung belly. They were definitely cat-like with furry ears and long blunt-ended tails, almost as if the tip had been chopped off. They were black, almost the colour of burning tyres, a sort of blue-black.' At least Mr Kingsley Newman's cats are consistent in appearance. Both are black leopard-like animals. However, in woods just a mile away Mr Mike Bronstow, exercising his Irish wolfhound, saw a large reddish-brown cat-like animal leap over a wall.

On the other side of Dartmoor, about 35 miles away, a number of people have seen large black panther-like cats over a number of years. Most of the sightings have been in the Tedburn St Mary area. But just a couple of miles up the road towards Crediton, people have been seeing a sandy or reddish-brown big cat. And in 1979, a few miles on the Dartmoor side of Tedburn, police and rangers launched a hunt for a lioness that was seen in the woods at Moretonhampstead.

Across the Cornish border, in June 1973, Mr David Nicholas was walking with a friend through Tehidy woods near Redruth when he saw a large puma-like cat walking ahead of them along the woodland path. This animal was a golden or tawny colour. But not far away Mr Berry of Penhalvean saw a large black panther-like animal during the autumn of 1980. Still, at least seven years separate the two sightings. Not so at Crowthorne in Berkshire. There Mr Alan J. Rogers saw a reddish-brown cat about the size of a red-setter dog but with a very long tail. Within days Mr and Mrs Paternoster of Camberley had also seen a large cat-like animal only 300yd from the same spot, but this animal was 'about the size of a Great Dane' and jet-black in colour.

The complications don't lessen as we travel north. In 1927 three 'large fierce yellow animals of unknown species' were killed in Inverness-shire. In 1974 a kind of lion was seen in Ayrshire. These animals all seem to be lion or puma coloured. But at Glenfarg in Perthshire in 1976 a large lynx-like cat with tufted ears was seen sitting on a garden wall. Also in 1976, in Sutherland, Alistair McLean saw a large cat-like animal of a dull rusty colour. And in Inverness-shire Miss Chisholm saw a beautiful pure black cat, larger than a Labrador dog. Next year she saw a much bigger black cat with white markings on its face and a long shiny-black tail, while a scientist working in the area reported seeing a large black leopard-like animal. In 1980 Miss Chisholm saw a dog-sized yellow cat with dark-brown rings or stripes! At Farr, Inverness-shire, in 1977, sightings were reported of a lioness and two cubs. In 1979, at Dingwall, reports were of a puma or lioness.

So what are we left with in the wilds of Scotland? Sandy or reddish-brown lionesses or pumas, black leopards or lynxes with tails. And we don't have black pumas, sandy leopards or tailed lynxes. Or do we?

There is one more piece of evidence to fit into the jigsaw. In Devon, Berkshire, Surrey, Inverness-shire, Sutherland and may counties in between, where cats have been seen, casts of pug-marks have been taken. Many of these have been confirmed by experts as cat prints, with one difference: they nearly all show claw-marks. And no big cat, other than the cheetah, shows claw-marks on its paw-print, because they all have retractable claws. And cheetahs, even if we had them, don't have black, sandy or reddish-brown coats, or tufted ears.

Why do all big cats, with just the one exception, sheathe their claws? The answer is simple enough. The cheetah, although it can climb trees, is basically a ground-living cat which relies on speed for hunting and to outrun its enemies. Therefore it does not need the razor-sharp claws that enable the other cats to grip when rapidly ascending or descending tree-trunks. The easiest way for these other cats to keep their essential claws needle-sharp is to carry them, like a well-honed knife-blade, in a sheath. But the evidence points to the British cats as being tree dwelling – at least not savannah or plains creatures, but animals of the woods and forests. So they need to sheathe those valuable claws. Why then, contrary to what might be expected from cat behaviour, do their pug-casts show clear claw-marks? As Mr Frost said of the animal he and his brother-in-law shot on Dartmoor in 1963: 'The feet were noticeably very powerful. Whether the claws were in or out in life I couldn't say, but certainly after it had died the claws were evident. They were quite definitely evident after it was dead.'

Summing up the cats reported over the years, from the northernmost forests of Scotland to the southernmost woods of Cornwall, three distinct types of animals have been described.

Type A A large black leopard-like cat with eyes that glow red in the dark. A forest- or wood-dwelling nocturnal hunter capable of bringing down a deer or a full-grown sheep. A cat with a glossy jet-black or charcoal-grey coat and thick blunt-ended long tail. Size between that of a spaniel and a Great Dane.

Type B A large brown cat-like animal resembling a lioness or a puma. Again a forest-dweller and a nocturnal hunter capable of killing and eating deer or sheep. Colour ranging from reddish-brown to ginger or golden-fawn. Sometimes showing spots or faint stripes. A long thick blunt-ended tail, possibly white-tipped. Size between that of a spaniel and a Great Dane.

These two animals could be colour variations of the same species – habitat, size and behaviour match. But what about the lynx? Mixed up with these other two animals are sightings of a spotted and striped yellow or fawny-brown cat with a long blunt-ended tail and tufted ears. Size about that of a spaniel dog. Again, forest-dwelling.

Type C The lynx. Could this be the juvenile of type B? All big cats, even the lion and puma, show spotted or striped coats as juveniles. So are the lynx-like cats the young of the large puma-like ones? And if types A and B are colour variations of the same animal, then the young black cats wouldn't show markings, but the reddish-brown or fawn cubs would. The tufted ears again could be either lost or unnoticed on the adult animals. The young of the cheetah, for instance, have a crest or ridge of long grey hair along their backs, but this is later lost.

Type D As the pattern emerges, is the picture complete? Not quite. The strange animal which Joan Gilbert saw in the early hours of the morning of April 1974, loping across the road at Branksome between Bournemouth and Poole, 'had stripes, a long thin tail and seemed to be all grey though it might have had some yellow on it'. And it will be remembered that she later chose a photograph of a thylacine or Tasmanian wolf – an animal that is sometimes called, because of a resemblance to a cat in body-shape, the Tasmanian tiger. Nor was she the only witness to identify the thylacine as nearest in appearance to the animal she had seen. Mr Peter Cookson had seen an animal resembling a Tasmanian wolf bound across a road in Kent, after Mr Fred Arnold had seen a similar animal in the same area.

In 1972 a number of people saw a large cat-like animal at Fleet in Hampshire. Dennis Long said it had a black head and a brown body with grey markings. Others agreed with his description. So we appear to have a fourth animal. This type D is a cat-like animal whose coat pattern resembles that of a tiger or a Tasmanian wolf. The ground-colour ranges from brown to yellow, with grey stripes.

Could these people by any chance have seen a Tasmanian wolf that was wandering around after escaping from captivity? The answer to that must be a definite 'no'. This animal is very nearly, if not entirely, extinct. Nor are there any breeds of dog with this colouration.

That brings us to another interesting animal that was seen by a large number of witnesses over almost a year. This was the Great Dog or 'Girt Dog' of Ennerdale. It was described as being a large smooth-coated animal with a lion-like tawny hide patterned with grey tiger-like stripes. It drew the wrath of the Lakeland farmers because of the large number of sheep it killed and ate, so it eventually signed its own death-warrant. Apart from the epithet 'dog' it sounds like the animal that Joan Gilbert and others saw in the early 1970s. And one witness to the 'Girt Dog' swore to his dying day that it wasn't a dog, but a lion.

Obviously it isn't the same individual animal for two reasons. Firstly, Ennerdale is hundreds of miles from Dorset and Kent. And secondly, the 'Girt Dog' of Ennerdale was killed on 12 September 1810, just over 160 years before Joan Gilbert saw her yellow-and-grey striped animal.

3

A Living Fossil?

What is a living fossil? Or perhaps first we should ask 'What is a fossil?' In the early nineteenth century a French scientist, Georges Cuvier, made astounding discoveries of giant mammal bones in the region of Paris. At the time it was generally believed that the earth was only thousands of years old, and it was the work begun by Cuvier and continuing to this day that tells such a different story. Before man appeared on the scene the great age of mammals had lasted for over 60 million years, and this is only a fraction of the time-scale of the earth itself. It might be wondered how we can judge this immensity of time. The rocks themselves yield the information from which geologists and palaeontologists calculate and build a picture of the past. An important part of this information is provided by fossils.

When an animal such as a rabbit dies, the chances of its body existing for more than a few days are very slight. Other animals and birds feed on the carrion, and tinier creatures like ants move in to pick clean the remains. Usually no record of the animal's existence is left except for a few scattered bones. But if a rabbit should, for instance, make the mistake of falling into a treacherous swamp and drowning, it would be quickly buried in mud or sand where no predators would tear its body apart, and if that sediment hardened – sometimes over millions of years – the body entombed within it would be preserved as a fossil. This is a very hit-and-miss affair, and obviously animals that live in swamps, or perhaps hibernate in cool caves, are more likely to be preserved than those that live on the savannah. None the less enough fossils are found to give scientists a reasonably comprehensive picture of the past. It can never be complete, for many creatures have a lifestyle that does not allow even a one-in-

99

a-million chance of their bodies being preserved. In fact some species are known only by teeth, for teeth were of no interest to carnivores, and did not decay like the soft parts before being buried.

So a fossil is the remains of a dead creature that through some freak chance has been preserved for thousands or even millions of years. A common mistake is to believe that fossils are necessarily the remains of extinct creatures. This is not true. Of course a large number of creatures are known to us only as fossils, the best known and spectacular of these being the great reptiles. But other creatures of which fossils have been found are still with us today, perhaps in a slightly altered form. These creatures are living fossils, a link between the Age of Reptiles and the Age of Mammals including man. It is convenient to talk of an Age of the Mammals, but the first mammal-like creatures existed during the Jurassic and Cretaceous eras at the same time as the reptiles, when monster dinosaurs walked the earth and the most terrifying of all predators, Tyrannosaurus, ruled. Hidden in the lush undergrowth of the vast rain forests, small rodent-like creatures scuttled about, and true birds fluttered overhead. Then came the great disaster and Tyrannosaurus ruled no more. The dinosaurs were dead and the mammals were ready to take over. But we still have creatures living today whose ancestors shared the vast swamps and forests of the Cretaceous period with the great dinosaurs, and who have changed little, if at all, over the 140 million years since then – frogs, salamanders, snakes, lizards, turtles and crocodiles.

Plants too have come down to us. At the beginning of the Tertiary period some 65 million years ago, a walk in the sub-tropical forests would have produced many of the trees that can be seen today, such as banana, palm, fig and even soapberry. And in the more temperate regions could be found great redwoods, oak, sycamore and the exotic-looking ginkgo. In the lakes and rivers were fish like sturgeon, garpike and bowfin, keeping the turtles and crocodiles company. In fact all these are living fossils – life that has shown little, or no change for, in some cases, over

100 million years. At that time it is thought that Europe and North America were linked by a land-route stretching from the British Isles across the Atlantic to Iceland. This is believed to account for the similarity between species on what are now different continents.

By the time of the Eocene, beginning 55 million years ago, the land masses of the world were beginning to resemble what they are today, though the British Isles was possibly still linked across the North Atlantic. The plants would be very familiar to a voyager in time. Tropical trees like the breadfruit grew alongside the ferns and palms; but also there were willow, walnut, birch, alder, hickory, maple and ash, to name just a few. With the redwoods were great pines, and flying about in the twilight above these forests were bats including the horseshoe bat, looking just as it does today. Lemurs also appeared. And an ornithologist would have felt at home, for the birds included herons, cranes, woodpeckers, ducks, owls, vultures, gulls, petrels, cormorants and even loons. In the swamps, terrapins joined the turtles. On land, lizards were joined by monitors, iguanas, slow-worms and python-like snakes. The insect world was beginning to make its mark. Crickets, grasshoppers, termites, cockroaches, sexton beetles, ground beetles, flourished and in the grass could be found glow-worms and even mealworms, whilst jewelled dragonflies swooped over the swamps. There was even the beautifully coloured, but now universally hated, bluebottle. At this time the land tortoises appeared, millions of years after their soulmates, the turtles. These reptiles, birds, trees and insects also truly merit the title of living fossils.

The Oligocene began 36 million years ago and land mammals such as hedgehogs, moles and shrews arrived, although the hedgehog family tree goes back to the Cretaceous days of the dinosaurs. And the true rhinoceros made its appearance, today called the Sumatra rhino. At this time, too, appeared the mammals of most interest to this investigation – the cats. The family had first appeared at the end of the Eocene period, but it was the Oligocene before the cats really established themselves and began to branch off into various species. The most spectacular of all were the early sabre-tooths, many of whom were heavy, clumsily built animals, using weight and power rather than speed or cunning to catch their prey, which seems to have consisted mainly of larger animals. But alongside these ferocious and powerful cats developed animals very much like our big cats of today, leopard-sized and with cat-like teeth of normal size.

Then 25 million years ago began the Miocene period. Africa was part of the main European land mass and the British Isles was still joined to Europe, but completely divided by the Atlantic from the North American continent. A hint of what was to come was provided by the beginning of glaciation in the Arctic and Antarctic regions. The first apes appeared. The cat family thrived, both sabre-tooths and modern types. And a small cat, the size of the European wild cat, appeared. This is the true cat of modern times – the genus *Felis*. Although so tiny compared to the lion-sized sabre-toothed Machaerodus, this little cat survived to provide us with all the cat species of modern times, one of which would one day earn the title of king of the beasts. And another seemingly insignificant event was taking place: the hominid *Ramapithecus* was spreading from the African continent, arriving just as the earth was about to enter the Pleistocene or Great Ice Age.

The Pleistocene or Ice Age lasted some 3 million years, but it was not 3 million years of continual ice sheet. It was more like a series of winters and summers. There were five of these long winters, each lasting many thousands of years and destroying large numbers of creatures. However the successful ones adapted and, like early man, thrived. One of the families that came into its own at this period was the cats. The cats and man evolved side by side. There were the mighty and grotesque true sabre-tooths, for example Smilodon, a great cat that hunted across America until as recently as 11,000 years ago. It was a massively built animal with powerful shoulders and deep chest, designed to hold down its prey whilst the huge sabre-shaped canines stabbed downwards. All the power and weight was in the front of the cat; the rear was slight with a short bob-tail. As already mentioned, the sabre-tooth was not designed for speed. Possibly we know more about this creature than any other of that time because it prowled about the famous La Brea tar pits, near Los Angeles. Probably attracted by the struggles of animals that became trapped in the sticky tar, the hunter in turn became the prey. To date nearly 2,500 fossils of Smilodon have been found in the tar beds.

There was a larger cat than the sabre-tooth in the region, however. This was *Panthera atrox*, the Great Cat. A quarter again as large as the largest tiger of today, this was a truly awesome creature – a lion-like modern cat, built for speed as well as power, with a formidable bite, although lacking the tremendous sabres of Smilodon. A close relative of this animal was the cave lion. This is the first of the past cats we can reconstruct without reliance on fossil evidence, because our own ancestors left a record in European caves. On the walls, painstakingly and beautifully painted, are pictures of the animals seen and hunted at the time. The cave lion is shown as maneless and sometimes striped. Also in existence over 2 million years ago were modern cats of the lynx and puma species. The leopard and cheetah also hunted over the whole of Europe. So if the Ice Age didn't destroy them, why did some cats such as Smilodon become extinct and others change their hunting territory?

The process of extinction lasted between 1,000 and 20,000 years depending on the area, and an average of 50 per cent of species was lost for ever – an incredible rate of destruction for species that had successfully evolved and survived for millions of years. And the cause of this dreadful destruction was not climatic change or volcanic upheaval, but the evolution of the great destroyer. Even Smilodon and the Great Cat had no chance against the ape-like creature with the greater brain. The destruction took two basic forms: direct through rivalry and indirect through interference with the food chain.

The direct method involved hunting and killing, a process that continues to this day. An African herdsman fails to see beauty in the lithe shape of the hunting leopard. He only sees the threat to his livestock and his own lifestyle, and therefore he takes the only course open to him for his own survival: he uses his cunning and ability to make weapons to trap and destroy his rival. He can also call on the help of his fellow herdsmen, and hunt in a pack. The leopard, for all its strength, speed and stealth, has no chance against such odds. So it was 10,000 years ago. Creatures that had had no cause for fear suddenly came up against an enemy from which they had no protection. Only the cunning survived, and they did so by moving their territories as far as possible from the hunting grounds of man. Or else they remained hidden, living secretive lives and leading a mainly nocturnal existence.

Man wasn't finished with his rivals. He had discovered fire and the many uses to which it could be put. One of these was for the clearing of land. This had two purposes: firstly the firing of certain areas drove from cover large amounts of game to the slaughter. Secondly, the fired land, now stripped of vegetation, could be used for grazing or agriculture. Although good for man, this was bad for other creatures. The wholesale slaughter of herds of wild animals made huge gaps in the food chain, often eventually destroying whole species completely; and the deforestation of large areas destroyed the habitat of many forest-dwelling creatures. Just what this means to an area of land is illustrated by what happened in the British Isles. Ten thousand years ago, at the end of the last glacial period, there were a great number of large mammals that cannot be seen today — mammoth, woolly rhino, musk ox, cave lion, cave panther, cave bear, cave hyena and scimitar cat. These animals are now extinct and it is very noticeable that the list includes a large number of cave-dwellers. It is no coincidence that man found caves useful as his first home and made a determined onslaught. Other animals now missing from our British fauna include the leopard, cheetah, lion and lynx; but just when did these die out? Remember how hit-and-miss our records are — the chance in a million of a creature's remains becoming fossilised. As with swamp-dwellers, the environment of cave-dwellers allows the possibility of fossilisation; but for plain or forest-dwelling animals the situation is different. If a leopard crawls away into the forest to die, within weeks if not days the scavengers will have done their work, as nature's dustmen. Nothing is left to tell us when the animal died, unless we happen at some time to dig up the teeth. We just don't know when the leopard, lion, lynx and cheetah died out. And as we do not know, we cannot really prove that they are indeed extinct. Remember that the lizards basking on the rocks and the frogs clustered around the garden pond have been with us for an unbelievable 65 million years; herons, ducks and owls have been with us for 50 million; and for 12 million years we have had modern-type cats. These time scales put into true perspective the short period of 10,000 years. So could a large cat have retreated into the wilds of the British Isles? What would it look like, how would it change over this period, if at all? What type of lifestyle would it have to evolve to escape from its only enemy, man?

To answer these questions we will invent a cat of average size – about that of a leopard. How would our average cat have lived through 10,000 years. If it was average, then it would not have evolved with a specialist form of killing-weapon such as sabre-teeth. It would be powerful, heavy enough to bring down prey that would probably be heavier than itself, but light enough to attain a good burst of speed when hunting. To our eyes it would look very much like a leopard or puma – neat, long-bodied, with powerful back legs for springing and muscular shoulders and neck for holding down and dragging or carrying its prey. Its method of killing would probably be the same as that of most big cats today. If a spring on to the back of its prey doesn't kill through snapping the neck, then the neck is gripped to produce death through strangulation.

Its colour would be very much determined by its environment. The leopard for instance does not have that beautifully spotted coat for aesthetic reasons. The spots reproduce the effect of

105

dappled sunlight on leaves, for the leopard spends most of its day sleeping amongst the leafy canopy high up in the trees. It is interesting that the Malayan leopard that lives in dark jungle conditions produces a high proportion of melanistic or black animals, whereas in the lighter foliage of the African bush, black colouring is very rare. The lion however is sandy or reddish-brown, because this is the best camouflage when lying in the dry, brownish grasslands of the African plains, or when sprawled along the bare brown branches of the scrub-trees and bushes. The tiger carries his magnificent stripes because of the tall spear-like jungle undergrowth and bamboo-like grasses of its environment. So to guess the colour of our imaginary surviving large cat, we must look closely at its environment. The flora of the British Isles hasn't changed much over the last 10,000 years; its distribution has altered, through agriculture. We certainly didn't have the lush tropical jungle foliage that gives the tiger its stripes, so our cat would not need such markings. It would be faced with living in two basic environments – grasslands not unlike the commons of today and the dark, partly coniferous, forests of the temperate climate. For the grasslands it would be either spotted like the African leopard or golden-brown like the lion. So which? The answer could lie in the New World rather than the Old. Parts of the United States of America are very like our British countryside, but on a much bigger scale. The prairies of a hundred years ago were like enormous commons, and the forests were like spacious and vast temperate woods. So how have their cats evolved – are they brown or spotted? The largest, a jaguar, is spotted like the leopard, but this hunts in the tropical jungles of the south, not the temperate north. In the north are three large cats – the puma, the lynx and the bobcat. The largest, the puma, is sometimes called the cougar or mountain lion, because it is the lion of the Americas. It is very like our 'average cat' in size, but unlike the leopard is a ground-loving animal. Although it does climb trees, it dens up in hollows and caves, very like the lion. But unlike the lion it is a solitary hunter, moving swiftly and quietly, its senses alert and highly developed, keeping hidden. As mentioned before, many wardens of national parks where pumas are known to live have never seen one. Like the lion, its coat is tawny or brown, an ideal colour for the plains. But unlike the lion it does not rely on weight and group-hunting activities; therefore it is of lighter build, with larger pricked ears – for as a mainly nocturnal hunter, its hearing is very acute. Although melanistic or black pumas are not unknown, they are rare. For although in the dark forests of Malaya black is a better camouflage, it has no real advantage in the airier and lighter forests of the United States. It would in fact be of disadvantage, in that it would restrict the animal's territorial range, for the American puma ranges from forests to plains and mountains.

So what can we learn from the puma with regard to our imaginary cat? It seems that the vividly spotted coat of the jaguar or leopard is only really of use in jungle, or where bright perpetual sunlight plays on leaves. Otherwise the brown or tawny colour seems very successful in a variety of environments and black is useful for a night hunter in dark forest.

Armed with this knowledge we look again at the British countryside. The centre flatlands are rather like the prairies on a smaller scale, so a tawny or brown colour might be best for concealment. But what about the British forests? The deciduous woodlands seem to invite the same colouration as the plains, but in our dark conifer forests, where sunlight seldom penetrates, dappled or spotted colouration would be wasted. Especially for a nocturnal hunter, black would appear to be a very useful guise in Britain, for few eyes could detect a black, swiftly moving shape amongst the dark shadows of a forest night. So our imaginary cat would probably need a brown coat if living on commons or in deciduous woods, and a black coat if living in the darker denser conifer forests.

It would also have a puma-like head with pricked, upright ears for sensitive hearing, for hearing is of greatest importance to a hunting cat. Sight comes second, but is not much use to a nocturnal hunter; the sense of smell is the least developed. So could our imaginary cat improve its hearing even more? To decide, we must look at another secretive cat, the lynx.

The cat has a very sensitive body. The whiskers are the most sensitive of all its hairs, for through them the animal can judge width, giving it the security of knowing that the passage through which it wishes to pass will take the full width of its body. It is this that enables the household cat to wriggle through seemingly impossibly small spaces. But there are other useful hairs. Lightly touch those on the ears of a sleeping cat and you will see instant reaction. Even if you just gently brush them with another hair, the result will be the same. So the hairs of the ears are sensitive, like the whiskers. If you look at the lynx, or its relatives the bobcat and the caracal, you see that these cats have developed the ear hairs into tufts, sensitive to any vibration – a very useful adaptation for a night hunter. So if our imaginary cat is a nocturnal hunter, tufted ears would greatly assist its night-time prowls.

To sum up, our imaginary cat would be about the size and build of a leopard; it would be tawny-gold, gold or russet-brown in colour, although if forest-dwelling it could produce a melanistic or black strain. If of nocturnal habit, it could have developed ear tufts.

So we have some idea what it would look like, but how would it have reacted to the arrival of man? Would it, like so many species, have become extinct, or would it move its territory? Moving territory is not easy when you are living on a small island; there are not so many places to move to. The first thing would be for it to leave the open ground and take to the trees. The second thing would be to make itself as inconspicuous as possible – keep away from caves where man has already staked his claim and retreat to the depths of the forest, or to the wild and least hospitable areas. There it would live a solitary life, meeting its own kind purely for mating purposes, otherwise hunting alone and silently, avoiding daylight, using the darkness for cover.

Our imaginary cat now has the requirements for survival in a hostile environment, unlike the cave-dwellers who tried to rival

Photograph taken in Tonmawr, Wales (see Chapter 5). This shows a large cat on the hillside in the centre of the picture. Note the cheetah-like shape, small head, long front legs and powerful hind quarters. The bare stump immediately below the cat is nearly 2 ft high (*Steve Joyce*)

Cub photographed in Tonmawr (see Chapter 5). Though only a cub, it is still much larger than a domestic cat, shown opposite in the same position. Note the cub's powerful shoulders and neck, puma-like head and claws used almost like fingers (*Steve Joyce*)

Domestic cat shown in the same position for comparison – it is actually nearer to the cabinet and the string is lower down (*Steve Joyce*)

Cub photographed from the rear, showing the back markings (*Steve Joyce*)

man, and the plain-dwellers who were a direct threat to man's livestock and therefore his own food chain. But for how long could this imaginary cat live on this overcrowded island without being seen? For 10,000 years certainly, but not for the last 100 years. Nothing man did in the past could be as disturbing as the invention of the car, with its unsocial habit of appearing suddenly in lonely country lanes, the bright beam of its headlights illuminating the dark verges. Our imaginary cat could not have prepared for this traumatic happening. Coupled to this intrusion into the wild places is their gradual total loss. Stretches of lonely woodland are now stretches of lonely concrete housing estates. Our cat would have fewer places in which to live, less chance of finding food and little chance of remaining unseen.

Let us now look at the cats people have reported seeing from all over the country. There are two basic colourations – brown or tawny (described as lion- or puma-like) and black – the two colourations that our imaginary cat would probably have evolved. Size is usually that of a leopard or puma; although smaller animals have been seen, either black or with spots running into stripes on a gold or brownish background. But the young of lion and puma show spots. 'Ears upright, puma-like', but often 'tufted or very hairy like a lynx'. Ear tufts could be developed to assist a nocturnal hunter. Where are they seen? Always near woods or forest areas, often in fairly wild lonely situations. The Scottish Highlands, the Welsh National Parks, the forests and woods about Dartmoor, are places of frequent sightings. As to when they are seen, a few are observed hunting or basking in the sunshine of late afternoon in isolated areas; but most sightings occur at night. A very large number are made by drivers who catch the animals in their headlights as they are crossing country roads or walking along verges – a method of discovery that could not have existed before the advent of the car. In fact it doesn't take much stretch of the imagination to replace our image of a cat that could have survived by a cat that appears to have actually done so. Appearance and apparent behaviour match. Only at mating time are two adult cats ever seen together, otherwise the only multiple sightings are of mothers with cubs. They live as isolated from man as possible and attempt to avoid all contact with him, to the point almost of cowardice. However provoked, they appear extremely reluctant to retaliate or attack a human being, almost as though their intelligence warns them that an attack on a man will mean in return an attack on them by men.

But could a cat exist in the British Isles that is different from any other existing cats: not just a British leopard or a British lynx, but one with characteristics of a number of other animals? An animal that is either the only survivor of a species that has been destroyed elsewhere, or one that has evolved in isolation over thousands of years to produce a species that is unique to the British Isles.

The easiest way to answer this question is to look again at existing cats and see whether such a unique survivor from the past can be found among them elsewhere – a living fossil. The beautiful clouded leopard is, in fact, such an animal. Its skull is much more elongated than that of other modern cats, who have evolved rounded skulls; it is very like that of the early cats. But it has an even more interesting feature that makes it a living fossil. It is a sabre-tooth, with huge canines like daggers that it uses to snatch monkeys and birds from the tree tops. Although not large as big cats go – the clouded leopard weighs only up to 50lb – it is strong enough and ferocious enough to kill wild boar and young buffalo. It lives deep in the forests of southern Asia and on the coastal islands including Borneo. It is seldom observed in its natural habitat, for it spends most of its time in the forest canopy where it is a master-acrobat, able to hang from the branches by one hind foot, monkey fashion, or travel upside-down along overhanging branches.

An even more exciting cat, though much smaller, is the iriomote. This little creature was only discovered in 1965 on Iriomote Island off Japan. Although still debatable, many zoologists believe that it is closely related to the extinct

Pseudaelurus, a cat dating back 25 million years and from which line came all the modern cats. The little iriomote shares some traits with the viverrids, which are believed to have produced both the cat and civet groups, as well as having similarities with Pseudaelurus. It is worth remembering that this little cat developed, isolated, in an island environment.

And another cat that stands alone in its environment is the beautiful but little-known snow leopard. Like the clouded, it is not a true leopard, but has gained the title because of its pale spotted coat. It lives on the high slopes of the mountains of central Asia and seldom descends below 5,000ft. So superbly is it adapted to its harsh existence that even its feet are furred. It is reputed to be able to make fantastic leaps from one rock to another, even turning somersaults in mid-air. How high or how far it can jump has never been recorded, but no zoo dare exhibit the animal in a moated or fenced enclosure.

So the answer to the question has to be 'Yes a unique cat could exist in the British Isles and, if it did, it would certainly look very much like the animal seen by so many witnesses over the years.' The only question left is not could it, but does it?

4

Black Dogs and Devil's Hoofprints

Perhaps one of the most important pieces of the jigsaw is to determine just how long the cats have been living and breeding in the British countryside. After all, if they have only been around in the wild for the last hundred years, they certainly aren't a new species or a separately evolved sub-species of an existing cat. But if it can be proved they have been around for the last thousand years, then they almost certainly are one or the other. But which, and how can it be proved anyway?

One factor that has emerged during my research in all areas is that although people are constantly spotting the animals, these sightings are seldom reported. There are a number of reasons for this apparent shyness. Firstly people are afraid that no one will believe them; that a statement that they have seen a black panther or lion-like animal will be greeted by howls of derision from family and friends, together with a well-meaning suggestion that the whisky bottle should be locked up. And the media too are, to say the least, sceptical. The pressure placed on witnesses is illustrated only too well by the following article which appeared in the *Herald Express* of Torbay on 11 January 1982 under the heading 'Looking for Big Cats'.

There has been some lament of late that the genuine English eccentric has apparently passed away. They were members of a small coterie who were looked on with indulgent affection by the community.

Then up pops Mrs Di Francis of Torquay. Convinced that there is a race of giant cats on Dartmoor, she is to spend the next few weeks out there in an attempt to find one. The reaction of most people will be one of admiration. Anybody who is prepared to live on

116

the Moor at this time of the year with the weather they will almost certainly face, deserves more than a passing salute. Nobody has ever reported seeing an outsize moggie on the Moor, but Mrs Francis is convinced that they are there and is ready to put up with something more than mere discomfort to find out.

They may of course, be there, just as maybe there is a monster in Loch Ness, a similar creature in New York harbour and a yeti or abominable snowman in the higher reaches of the Himalayas.

Just because nobody has actually seen and identified one is no proof that they do not exist. And we can all, in the last few years, remember when various experts have been forced to eat their words.

Nobody, we might suspect, would be more surprised than Mrs Francis if she actually meets a giant cat, but by going to find out she joins a select band that has delighted us through the years.

Perhaps the reporter responsible for the article also joins a select band, that of reporters who don't get their facts right. Just flick back to the pages in this book concerned with Devon sightings to see whether it is true that nobody has ever reported seeing outsize moggies on the moor. The police at Exeter and Okehampton might question that statement. But what really seems strange is that the same newspaper, just nine months before, had carried headlines about Mr Kingsley Newman seeing his black panther-type animals, together with a photograph of his daughters holding the casts of their cat-like prints.

But although many people are understandably nervous of coming forward to say they've seen large cats wild in Britain, some do have the courage to stand up and be counted. And research reveals such witnesses in the past. Sixteenth-century chronicler Ralph Holinshed's 'Lions we have had very many in the north parts of Scotland', has already been quoted, as has William Cobbett's record in 1830 of seeing a 'cat as big as a middle-sized spaniel dog, which went up into a hollow elm tree' near Farnham. But compared to the hundreds received this century, two over a period of about 400 years are very few indeed.

Is it possible that people did see large cats, but because of a lack of familiarity with such animals, or a lack of adequate lighting, or even because of superstitious fear, did not recognise the animals for what they were? With this in mind I began to examine closely a number of 'Black Dog' sightings. Black Dogs were considered by many before the turn of the century to be companions of the devil, or even the devil himself in another guise. Certain areas throughout the British Isles were known and feared because of their association with these terrifying encounters. Was it possible that the stories recorded not meetings with the devil, nor even flesh-and-blood dogs, but chance encounters with a large hunting cat?

A story from *The Middle Kingdom* by D. A. MacManus illustrates my point. The scene is County Londonderry in Northern Ireland, a country that has both Black Dog and modern black cat sightings, but which is not covered by this book. At Easter 1928 a student of Trinity College, Dublin, was standing on the edge of a gravelly small pool in a river bed, fishing. He suddenly saw a 'huge black animal come into sight, padding along in the shallow water. He could not at first make out what it was, whether dog, panther or what, but he felt it to be intensely menacing.' Frightened, he climbed a tree.

> Meanwhile the animal continued padding steadily along and as it passed it looked up at him with almost human intelligence and bared its teeth with a mixture of a snarl and a jeering grin. His flesh crept as he stared back into its fearsome blazing red eyes which seemed like live coals inside the monstrous head. Even so, he could only think of it as a wild savage animal which had presumably escaped from some travelling circus. It passed on and was soon lost to view.

Assuming that the student was neither lying nor hallucinating, what did he really see? The most important words are 'whether dog, panther or what'. The witness, a university student, seeing the animal for a few minutes from an extremely close vantage-point, couldn't be sure. How much more difficult identification would be for an uneducated farm worker, whose life was filled with superstition. Certainly the slow padding movement would appear to be like the plod of a big cat. 'Blazing red eyes' and 'live coals' are both phrases that have been used by modern witnesses to describe cats' eyes, and the mixture of 'a snarl and a jeering grin' could well describe the expression on the face of a prowling big cat. Also typical is the tendency to stare unabashed for a few moments before deciding that whatever had attracted its attention wasn't really worth any further effort. Analysis of the story points to the creature being of the feline variety rather than the canine. And there is nothing to suggest that the animal was anything other than of this world, either cooling its paws or else, like the human, fishing.

Can we prove anything by examining the stories of the past? No, but circumstantial evidence suggests that the animals were neither dogs nor ghosts, but simply big cats such as are being seen today. If for instance the counties that produce Black Dog legends also have present-day big cats, and the areas where they are seen and the circumstances under which they are sighted match, then we have, if nothing else, food for thought.

Starting in the north of the British Isles, in Sutherland, Scotland, where there have been so many modern cat sightings, there is the Black Dog of Creag an Ordain that is supposed to have been seen splashing out of a loch. Further south at Carn Mor near Loch Tay, Perthshire, a huge Grey Dog appears at another waterside haunt, while the Dog o'Mause appears some 20 miles to the east at Blairgowrie. Caisteal a Choin Dubh, the Castle of the Black Dog, is so called because of the Black Dog that was seen in the area. At Knapdale, Argyllshire, is Dun a Choin Dubh, the Fort of the Black Dog. Unfortunately, this gives us very little information, although it does record past sightings.

Across the English border in Yorkshire there were so many sightings of the Black Dog of Kettleness that in the 1950s the Reverend Dr Donald Omand was asked to exorcise the animal. And Yorkshire, it will be remembered, produced a modern cat sighting at Thorganby.

Lancashire produces a much more interesting animal for our purposes. Its Black Dog has the honour of having two names —

Shriker or Trash – both names given because of the noises heard in association with it. Trash is because its footsteps are supposed to sound like heavy shoes splashing along a muddy road – which brings to mind the sawing-wood sound a pacing leopard makes. Shriker is because of the terrible screams it makes. It is also believed to have a habit of walking backwards ahead of witnesses. I'm not sure where the walking backwards fits in, unless the animal is backing off from the encounter, but certainly such screams are much more in keeping with a cat than a dog. Scottish witnesses described the cat as sounding like a woman screaming, and Surrey witnesses likened the sound to a thousand cats being murdered at the one time.

Lincolnshire is another interesting county. Although my only records of cat sightings are in the Skegness area, it has a number of Black Dog legends. The sightings are as follows:

Early this century a youth who cycled from Leverton to Wrangle reported he 'often saw the Black Dog rush out of a drove-end behind him and lope along to another lane which it turned down'. It is interesting to note the description of the animal's movement as a 'lope'. This is much more characteristic of a cat than of a dog.

A Black Dog that was seen regularly in Bourne Wood always disappeared at the same point, 'at a certain handgate at a corner of the wood'. Another creature of habit, the Dog of Moortown Hall, near South Valley, 'always appeared in the hedge at the same place'. The Black Dog of South Kelsey was always seen walking along a road adjacent to a small plantation. At Algarkirk the Black Dog was always seen near a clump of trees. An even more tree-loving animal was the Dog at Willoughton, which was frequently seen along a stretch of road beside a fish pond, and used to disappear by an ash tree. In fact one witness declared that the creature actually vanished 'up the tree or into the tree'.

Water seems to be another passion for the beast. A Black Dog was believed to at one time live in a burrow in a bank of a stream at Belle Hole Farm near Kirton. One haunts a culvert where a

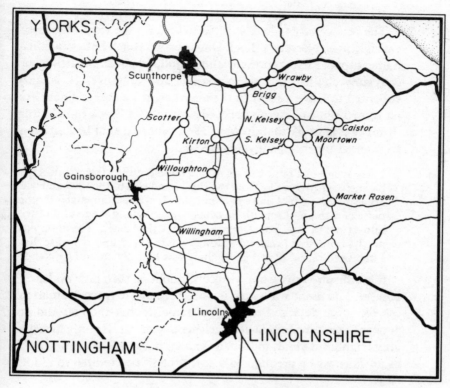

Map 5 Black Dog sightings in Lincolnshire

stream passes under the Wrawby road just outside Brigg. Another haunts a stream and the bridge crossing from Manton to Scotter along a 'green lane'. The Willingham Black Dog has a liking for the bridge crossing the River Till.

I felt that Lincolnshire was a suitable area to test a theory. I have no knowledge of the county, never having lived there, but if my theory was correct, a number of these sightings should have taken place within the area of a cat's territory of about 5 square miles. On a map of Lincolnshire I marked in the sightings. Willoughton, Kelsey, Moortown, Brigg and Scotter made an imperfect but noticeable circle about the size of a cat's hunting area.

The next county to look at is Norfolk, again the scene of modern cat sightings. Norfolk's Black Dog is called Black Shuck, again a name supposed to represent the sound, likened to rattling or dragging chains, that accompanies the creature. It is also supposed to leave a scent in the air where it has been. There are on record some modern supposed sightings of Black Shuck. For instance a Norfolk man in May 1945 reported that he had been frightened by the spirit dog. He said:

> I was aware of a faint baying as of a hound, after a few minutes the baying seemed to come from the right hand side of the road and was even louder, in fact quite ear-splitting. It was accompanied by the noise of a chain or something being dragged along the road. I broke into a run but after a few minutes I had to slow down. The noise was much fainter and I realised that this was the first time in my life that I had been afraid of a dog, my hair was literally standing on end.

It is difficult to draw any firm conclusions on such little evidence, and since no name was given it would be hard to trace the man to ask for more details. But the fact remains that the man didn't appear to see any animal at all, either dog or cat. He only heard a very frightening and, to him, unknown noise. If the sound can't in all fairness be credited to a cat, it can't be credited to a dog either.

The Birstall Black Dog of Leicestershire is locally believed to have lived in a pit known as Shag Dog Pit. But we have no records of cats in the county, and perhaps a flesh-and-blood dog really did once make its home there.

Nor are there records of Black Dog legends for Warwickshire – or of cats; but we have one interesting fact. In May 1977 a large 'black dog' ripped open the door of a rabbit hutch in a garden at Coventry. It was seen taking the rabbits and was chased and trapped in a garden shed; however it was heavy and powerful enough to force open a second door through which it escaped. Surely it would be very unusual behaviour in a dog firstly to rip open a hutch and secondly to force open a shed door? Most dogs guilty of attacking and killing pet rabbits do so when they find hutch catches unfastened, having neither the inclination nor the ability to force open the door. And usually once a dog is secured in an enclosed space, it is helpless. Again, like the Norfolk man's story, this one isn't firm evidence, but it provides food for thought.

. Herefordshire gives us a good example of typical Black Dog behaviour. Its Demon Dog of Hergest Court has been seen regularly near a pond by the road from Kington.

Hertfordshire has several reported Black Dogs, at Six Hills at Stevenage. One queries whether ghosts breed! And Buckinghamshire has a Black Dog that patrols the road between Stewkley and Soulbury, always disappearing before it reaches Soulbury.

Wiltshire, a county steeped in superstition and prehistoric remains, boasts two barrows that have ghost-dog connections. One, Doghill Barrow near Stonehenge, is reputed to be haunted by a Black Dog, and West Kennet Barrow and the Devil's Den at Fyfield to be haunted by light-coloured dogs. Somerset is also haunted by a Black Dog at Wambarrows, Winsford.

The dog legends really come into their own in the West Country, when you reach Devon. Here, on the lonely stretches of Dartmoor, was born the most famous of all Devil Dogs – the Hound of the Baskervilles; but its cousins are everywhere you care to look.

Torrington, in mid-Devon, for instance has a Black Dog that really believes in exercise. It is seen between Morchard Bishop and Winkleigh, between Blackditch Copse and Hollymoor Cross. Either the same one or a relative is believed to walk between Copplestone and Great Torrington, following the roads and ancient trackways. It has also been seen and heard in Down St Mary and on the lanes on either side. At Hollocombe, on Wyke Hill, it bays like a pack of hounds. Witnesses have described it as black, the size of a calf, and with glowing or shining eyes. Taking into account that this area has a number of black-panther sightings and that the Black Dogs are reputed to have been seen in living memory, one can't help but suspect that possibly the Black Dogs and the Black Cats come from the same parentage.

A large Black Dog is supposed to haunt the Tavistock to Okehampton road. Again this is cat country. At Postbridge a Black Dog as big as a donkey patrols the village at night and once jumped over a wall in front of a man. The jumping over the wall and the nocturnal habits could also apply to a cat, but I'm not so sure about the size: a dog would hardly be that size either.

Daddy Hole Plain at Torquay, according to legend, was once the home of two huge black hounds representing the devil's pack and they 'sounded in the wind as one hound'. And while it's true that Torquay could hardly house big cats or devil hounds today, years ago the woods would have reached right across to the Daddy Hole Plain area.

A more recent and puzzling Black Dog was the one seen by several people in Bradworthy about seventy years ago. Its movements, described as swift and silent, could certainly be those of a cat, but even cats have heads and this animal was described as headless. A hunting cat will often carry its head sunk between its shoulders in a typical stalking manner. It could possibly, in the dark, appear to be an animal without a head if the witnesses were looking for a head carried above the shoulders as a dog normally does.

Another strange happening within living memory occurred in Bradford also near Holsworthy. About fifty years ago there were sightings of a big ghost dog at night. A local man boasted 'he wasn't afeared of ghost dogs' and went to the place to wait for it. He kept on trying to persuade himself that it would not come, but it did. He whistled and called to it to come to him, whereupon it turned its great eyes on him and 'made the awfullest noise'. A lot of big-cat witnesses have remarked on the glowing eyes and the dreadful sound. Some twenty-five miles away, at Chittlehampton, a Black Dog runs along the Hudscott Plain at midnight; and at Frithelstock in 1932 one haunted a new road.

Finally over the Cornish border, Bodmin Moor has its own Black Dog. And near Launceston, where there have been cat sightings, a Black Dog once appeared to a group of wrestlers at Whiteborough.

So could Black Dogs be Black Cats? I don't think there is much doubt that in some cases, if not all, they certainly are. They are seen along the same stretches of country again and again, as though patrolling the area. This is consistent with cats hunting night after night in their own territories. Their eyes often blaze red — cats' eyes certainly do this. They snarl, howl, bay and scream, but never bark; and the description used by more than one witness that the Black Dog bayed like a hound could be recording a number of most undoglike noises. Black Dogs are constantly seen near woods, as are the cats. They are also frequently near water, and this too applies to cats.

Think again about the Dublin student: he could not at first make out what it was, whether dog, panther or what. And later he seems to have eliminated a dog from his list of possibilities because 'he could only think of it as a wild savage animal which had presumably escaped from some travelling circus'. Not a situation one would associate with a dog.

So much for the legendary dogs of Scotland and England. The Celtic land of Wales, not surprisingly, has produced many ghost stories, among them a number of Devil Hounds. For some of the best documented sightings we have to thank a Reverend Edmund Jones of Tranch Newport. He collected the stories in a book imposingly titled *A Relation of Apparitions of Spirits in the County of Monmouth and the Principality of Wales*, published in 1813. The sightings are recorded with such a care for detail that the statements of witnesses can be examined as though they had been made within the last couple of years. According to the reverend gentleman, the following was related to him by R. A., 'a true living experimental Christian'. In his words:

> As she was going to Laugharn town, Carmarthenshire, one evening on some business, it being late, her mother dissuaded her from going, telling her it was late and that she would be benighted; likely she might be terrified by an apparition which was both heard and seen by many and by her father among others, at a place called Pant y Madog, which was a pit by the side of the lane leading to Laugharn, filled with water and not quite dry in the summer.

However she seemed not to be afraid, therefore went to Laugharn. On coming back before night, though it was rather dark, she passed by the place; but not without thinking of the apparition: but being a little beyond this pit, in a field where there was a little rill of water and just going to pass it, having one foot stretched over it and looking before her, she saw something like a great Dog, one of the Dogs of Hell, coming towards her; being within four or five yards of her, it stopped, sat down and set up such a scream so horrible, so loud and so strong, that she thought the earth moved under her; with which she fainted.

There is little doubt that the animal described is more cat than dog. It behaved like the cat that Alan Pestell met in Thorganby and which sat and looked at him with its right paw lifted. And the scream is the sound that so many cat witnesses have tried to describe.

Another story in the same book comes from Pembrokeshire. A Mr W:

. . . went with a strong fighting Mastiff Dog with him; but suddenly he saw another Mastiff Dog coming towards him. He thought to set his own dog at it but his dog seemed to be much frightened and would not go near it. Mr W. then stooped down to take up a stone thinking to throw it but suddenly there came a fire round it so that he could perceive it had a white tail and a white snip down his nose and saw his teeth grinning at him; he then knew that it was one of the Infernal Dogs of Hell.

I'm not sure that the fire came from anywhere other than the furnace of Mr W's own fear and superstition, but his dog's reaction was typical of that of most dogs in the presence of a cat. And, like Miss Chisholm's cat in Scotland, some cats do show a flash of white on the face. And once again we recall the Dublin student's description that it 'bared its teeth with a mixture of a snarl and a jeering grin'.

Another story that originated in the 1830s, but wasn't recorded until it was written down by the grandson of the man in question for Ethel Rudkin who collected Folklore in 1936, concerned an event in Pembrokeshire:

At Redhill, four miles from Haverfordwest, at the point where a small brook, the Keystone, crosses the Mathry Road to join the Western Cleddau. On the northern side of the little bridge over the brook towards a rather dense growth of trees crowning a miniature cliff. Some three miles further north is the little village of Camrose. At the time of the described incident, my grandfather was the acting steward of the considerable estate of Camrose and his journeys to the neighbouring town of Haverfordwest were fairly frequent and always on foot. So far as I recollect the story, it was on his way home from Haverfordwest in the darkening evening that he became somewhat alarmed by a considerable commotion in the wood. In his pastoral mind, this could only be caused by a battle royal between some domestic animals and he wondered whose bull had invaded the territory of his neighbour and what dogs were joining in the melée. However, he was secure enough in the protection of the hedges and it seemed unlikely that the strife would culminate in the vanquished being forced through the thick trees to a drop over the crest of the little cliff into the brook beneath. A few yards walking brought him to the bridge and here he was terrified to see a huge black dog rise over the trees with a frightful roar and swoop downwards within a few feet of him, to the stream beyond the bridge.

One can't imagine a dog would 'rise over the trees with a frightful roar and swoop downwards,' but certainly a cat after a mating or territorial dispute might well do exactly that. Remember these cats can clear 10–11ft with ease from a ground position. A leap from the height of the trees would present no problem, and the 'frightful roar' is definitely a big-cat rather than a dog sound.

And other Black Dog sightings are recorded in the Haverfordwest area. J. W. Phillips wrote in 1920:

A Black Dog haunts part of the road from Haverfordwest to Pembroke Ferry about two miles outside the former town. The country people say there is 'fear' at that particular part of the road and do not care to pass there at night. I know of at least five persons who have seen the creature and all describe it as a large black creature between a dog and a calf in appearance. One man met it at 2 o'clock in the morning when on his way to fetch a doctor. I have myself seen it on two occasions.

And in the Pembroke Dock area, also near Haverfordwest, a woman spotted a large black Labrador-type dog running off with her rabbit in its mouth, having ripped off the wire-netting to get at the animal. This occurred as recently as mid-August 1976. A year before the same thing happened in Coventry and a year after I lost chickens in a similar fashion in Cornwall. Finally in the Vale of Glamorgan a Black Dog is said to follow people and snarl and growl at anyone who attempts to turn back; and in Gwent a Black Dog was seen going nine times round a tree at Trelleck.

So are — and were — Black Dogs real dogs with unusual behaviour patterns, or are they truly ghosts and companions to the devil? Or are some, if not all, flesh-and-blood big cats, the same as are being seen all over the country today? These are the questions we set out to investigate. There is strong evidence that the answer to the third query should be 'Yes'.

There is another dog that deserves more than a passing thought for, although legendary, this animal was definitely of the flesh, blood and voracious appetite type. It is remembered in folklore as the Girt Dog of Ennerdale. The animal first made its presence felt when a Cumberland farmer went to check his flock one spring morning in 1810. On the fells above Ennerdale Water he found that a predator had been amongst his sheep. The following day it was the turn of another flock, and night after night sheep were killed throughout the vale. The shepherds and farmers were on the alert for a rogue dog, for a fox could never have been responsible for the carnage. However, despite all-night vigils on the hillsides and attempts to trace and track the animal, the farmers had this time met their match. Whatever they were up against seemed to have extraordinary intelligence and cunning and continued its raids, never appearing to attack the same flock on two nights running. Its hunting ground covered enormous distances, for it raided fell and valley flocks alike and there was no way to foretell where it would strike next.

Then at last it was seen: at dawn a shepherd spotted it running down a large ramp. It was like no other animal the shepherd had ever seen — a very large tawny-yellow lion-like creature, its smooth coat patterned with dark-grey tiger-like stripes. The animal became the talk of the dales, everyone giving their opinion as to what it must be. Some said it was a lion, others that it was only a cross between a mastiff and a greyhound; yet others declared that it was no ordinary animal, but a supernatural beast. Whatever it was, the creature continued its nightly raids on the sheep. It seemed to travel great distances with amazing speed, to be in more than one place at once, and it never uttered any kind of sound. Killing was done swiftly and silently, always during the night or at dawn; despite desperate searches, no clue was ever left to guide people to the place where the animal was lying up during the day. Another thing that unnerved the farmers was the behaviour of dogs that got within range of it. The sheepdogs were a hardy, courageous breed, used to obeying every command of their masters, but close proximity to the Girt Dog had them cringing with terror. No ordinary dog would give chase. But by summer the farmers had put together a pack of hounds and at last the hunt was on. The tawny grey-striped beast broke cover and gave them a tremendous run at great speed; then, appearing to tire of the whole thing, it stopped and turned to face its attackers. The first hounds were dealt with swiftly and conclusively, and the hunters had the humiliating experience of seeing their prize pack turn tail and run.

After this, poisoned carcases were left on the hillsides, but the Girt Dog was no one's fool; it left the bait alone and continued to dine on the flocks of plump Ennerdale sheep. It also showed a tendency to drink the blood of its prey, vampire fashion, which did nothing to lessen the fear of the local people at having such a creature loose in the surrounding countryside. Rewards were offered and the men always carried guns with them, but still the Girt Dog plundered the hillsides. The dales were full of tales of courage and near-misses. A Willy Jackson, for instance, suddenly came face to face with the Girt Dog, finding it studying him calmly from a distance of only 30yd. Willy took a shot but the Girt Dog sloped off without uttering a sound. An even closer encounter concerned a deaf old man named Jack Wilson. Jack was described as being very old and bent, with legs so bowed that 'you could run a wheelbarrow through 'em'. One day he was gathering firewood and, being so deaf, wasn't aware that about thirteen men had closed in on the Girt Dog and had it apparently trapped in a nearby field of corn. As they tightened the circle, guns cocked, the Girt Dog made a break for freedom, dashing towards a man called Will Rotherby. Will decided that discretion was the better part of valour, and with a scream of 'Skerse! What a dog!' leapt sideways to safety. But old Jack, unaware of all the excitement, didn't have the same opportunity. The Girt Dog charged straight between his legs, tossing him through the air. The old man, having recovered from his undignified somersault, swore ever after that what had charged him had been no dog but a lion! Until his dying day, no one could shake him from his story that the Girt Dog was in fact a Girt Cat.

Regular packs of hounds with experienced huntsmen were now called in, and the Girt Dog provided them with runs that became folklore in hunting circles. For instance one such run started early in the morning with 200 riders. The hounds picked up the scent on Kinniside Fell and chased the quarry to Wastwater. From there the hunt continued to Calder, then to Seascale, being called off when it was dark, the chase having lasted all day. Another day the hunt met on Sunday morning and, when the hounds gave cry, all attending the service at Ennerdale church heard it. Within minutes the congregation was on its way and the church empty of man – even the parson joined in. The Girt Dog led them to Cockermouth, but there a violent thunderstorm put an end to the chase. Another day it led them from Ennerdale to St Bees, and on that occasion, as the weary pursuers were trudging fruitlessly home, the Girt Dog was observed quietly following them.

However, the Girt Dog was no supernatural animal and, in the way of all flesh, the end had to come. On 12 September 1810 it was surrounded, shot and wounded. Despite its injuries, the hounds still would not tackle it, so it was tracked down to the

Enen river where it cooled its wounds in the water. It made one last but futile bid for freedom in Eskat Woods, but was flushed out and shot again, after which the hounds took courage and finished it off. So ended a legend. The body is supposed to have been stuffed and put on exhibition in Keswick museum, but this was closed in 1876 and there is no record of the body being preserved. Indeed it is doubtful whether there would be anything of the body left after the hounds had completed their work.

Although the Girt Dog has gone down in legend as exactly that, it is difficult not to suspect that old Jack Wilson, the man who came closest of all to the beast, was right – that it was indeed a great cat, not a dog. It certainly was very like the grey-and-yellow-striped animal that witnesses in Dorset and Kent identified as a cross between a cat and a Tasmanian wolf, and its behaviour was very like that of our modern hunting cats. I've spent some time in sheep country where the cats are, and the Girt Dog's method of killing, its speed and even its vampiric habit, match exactly, as does the total lack of aggression towards man unless cornered. And as Donald Bruce of Sutherland said: 'There now seems to be a pattern over a wide area which suggests there could be more than one animal.' That could explain the Girt Dog being in two places so far apart on the same night.

There is another legend that interested me during my research, and that makes it possible that the cats could offer a solution to a hitherto insoluble mystery. In 1855 the county of Devon was in an uproar of superstitious fear. The newspapers and letters of the time tell the story, a report in *The Times* on 16 February being the first publicising of the mystery.

Considerable sensation has been evoked in the towns of Topsham, Lympstone, Exmouth, Teignmouth and Dawlish, in the south of Devon, in consequence of the discovery of a vast number of foot-tracks of a most strange and mysterious description. The superstitious go so far as to believe that they are the marks of Satan himself; and that great excitement has been produced among all classes may be judged from the fact that the subject has been descanted on from the pulpit.

It appears that on Thursday night last [8 February] there was a very heavy fall of snow in the neighbourhood of Exeter and the south of Devon. On the following morning the inhabitants of the above towns were surprised at discovering the tracks of some strange and mysterious animal, endowed with the power of ubiquity, as the footsteps were to be seen in all kinds of inaccessible places, on the tops of houses and narrow walls, in gardens and courtyards enclosed by high walls and palings as well as in open fields. There was hardly a garden in Lympstone where the footprints were not observed.

The track appeared more like that of a biped than a quadruped, and the steps were generally eight inches in advance of each other. The impressions of the feet closely resembled that of a donkey's shoe, and measured from an inch and a half to two and a half inches across. Here and there it appeared as if cloven, but in the generality of the steps the shoe was continuous and, from the snow in the centre remaining entire, merely showing the outer crest of the foot, it must have been convex.

The creature seems to have approached the doors of several houses and then to have retreated, but no one has been able to discover the standing or resting point of the mysterious visitor . . .

At present it remains a mystery and many superstitious people in the above towns are actually afraid to go outside their doors after night.

Woolmer's Exeter and Plymouth Gazette of 17 February states that the night of 8 February, the night before the appearance of the footsteps, was marked by a heavy fall of snow, followed by rain, boisterous wind from the east, and frost. All weather reports indicate an exceptionally severe winter. The paper reaffirms what *The Times* had said as to size, spacing and conformation of the foot-tracks, only adding that they could be included between two parallel lines 6in apart.

Letters from private persons began to appear. According to Mr D. Urban:

The marks, to all appearances, were the perfect impression of a donkey's hoof, the length four inches by two and three quarter inches, but instead of progressing as that animal would have done, or indeed as any other would have done, feet right and left, it appeared that foot had followed foot, in a single line; the distance from each tread being eight inches or rather more ... This mysterious visitor generally only passed once down or across each garden or courtyard and did so in nearly all the houses in many parts of several towns ... also in the farms scattered about; this regular track passing in some instances over the roofs of houses and hayricks and very high walls, without displacing the snow on either side or altering the distance between the feet and passing on as if the wall had not been any impediment.

The Reverend G. M. Musgrave studied the tracks and recorded that they 'climbed over roofs, under bushes eight inches from the ground and even disappeared into a six inch drainpipe to emerge at the other end and then finally stopped dead in the middle of a field'. He wrote to the *Illustrated London News* that 'the labourers ... their wives and children and old crones, and trembling old men' would not venture out of doors after dark or 'go out half a mile into lanes or byways on a call or message, under the conviction that this was the Devil's walk and none other and that it was wicked to trifle with such a manifest proof of the Great Enemy's immediate presence'.

He also sent sketches of the hoofprints to be published in the *Illustrated London News* and suggested that the marks could have been made by a kangaroo. This prolific writer even wrote a poem based on the fact that a neighbouring parson had a dog's paw-marks all over his roof and had accused the author's Newfoundland dog, now dead seventeen years.

An even more outrageous suggestion was made by naturalist Sir Richard Owen, who studied Musgrave's drawings and offered the opinion that the tracks were those of a badger, ignoring the discrepancy in the measurements of the tracks, even taking into consideration distortion by melting snow.

Mr H. T. Ellacombe of Clyst St George sent the following letter to the *Illustrated London News* with a request that it should not be published:

The marks as of one creature were on my own premises, across a lawn round the house to a Pump Shed. These were visible three days afterwards. My dog barked that night and so did the dogs of my neighbours where marks were seen. There is scarcely a field or an orchard or garden where they were not, all in a single line, under hedges; in one field near me, a turning round and doubling appeared. Two neighbours who followed the tracks thro' the same field in the snow, met with excrement and there the tracks were spread, doubled but afterwards single.

A note on the excrementa described four oblong lobes of a whitish colour the size and shape of a large grape. Also at Clyst St George, according to a Mr H. T. Ellacombe, the trail led up to the outside of a Mr Dovetan's closed garden door, then appeared on the inside of it and ran all round the garden. To do this it must have hopped an 8ft wall.

Most sightings were made over a period of four days. The majority of reports gave the prints as 2½in wide and 4in long; some were like a donkey's, some cloven and some said to show claws. They were clearly defined in towns and villages along both sides of the Exe estuary and slightly inland. At one place it was said that the tracks appeared suddenly in the middle of a field, and at Dawlish the local hunt attempted to follow tracks, but the hounds returned baying and terrified of something they found or scented in a wood. All this became known as the Devil's Hoofprints Mystery.

As is usual with such accounts, one has to sift through a great deal of conflicting hearsay and superstition to examine the real nature of the incident. Firstly, 1855 was not the first time such prints had been observed. Around 1850, again following a severe winter, similar prints were seen in Devon; but these did not hit the headlines and were quietly forgotten. Secondly, the prints did not all appear in one night. The tracks at Topsham were not seen until 14 February, several days after the first reports, which were on 8 February, so the prints were either made by an animal that took six days to travel the distance attributed to it in one night, or else were made by several animals, and the track was not linked by anything more than human imagination. (If indeed the prints were all made by the same species, if not the same individual animal.)

Commonsense tells us that, after the first burst of publicity, everything that had made a track of any description would run the risk of being identified with the devil. Certainly a number of the tracks would have been made by nothing more terrifying than the local cattle or a neighbour's donkey. And it's fairly safe to ignore prints such as those reported by Reverend Musgrave that 'disappeared into a six inch drainpipe to emerge at the other end'. I've also attempted to identify the 'excrementa' mentioned by Mr Ellacombe and I doubt very much if the grape-sized lobes were passed by anything larger than a fox. In fact fox-droppings mixed with rabbit fur do resemble those found by Mr Ellacombe. But a fox couldn't leave footprints $2\frac{1}{2}$in across by nearly 4in.

What did the prints look like? Some were like cloven hoofs, others were showing claws. Neither donkeys nor dogs could follow the route that the creature or creatures appeared to take, passing in some instances 'over the roofs of houses and hayricks and very high walls, without displacing the snow on either side or altering the distance between the feet and passing on as if the wall had not been any impediment'. However a large cat could do this, with little difficulty. And melting snow would certainly distort many of the prints made.

As an experiment, I made a series of prints in snow from a cast of one of the cat's pug-marks, obtained in Devon. The results were interesting. With little change, the prints could resemble both a donkey's and a cloven hoof. And a cat has a tendency to walk with its relaxed paws almost crossing under its body, which can make the track look as if it has been made by a biped, rather than by a dog, which keeps its four paws rigidly apart with clear spacing between.

So if it's possible that a big cat made the mysterious footprints of 1850 and 1855, why did it do so? Both sightings of tracks occurred after particularly bad weather and food would be scarce. Just as the leopard does in Nairobi, it might find that the best place to search for food was around human habitations. Remember the large cat-like animal that was reported to have forced open a dustbin at Drumnadrochit, Inverness-shire? And

Miss Lesley Bryant reported seeing a cat about the size of a Great Dane going through the farm's rubbish bags near Crediton in Devon. So perhaps the devil was really a desperately hungry cat in search of food, whether a farmyard hen or a bone on the garbage heap.

If so, wouldn't such tracks in the snow have appeared in other places? In Scotland in 1840, similar tracks were recorded 'among the mountains where Glenorchy, Glenlyon and Glenochay are contiguous'. And in 1855, at the same time as the Devil's Hoofmarks appeared in Devon, similar prints were noted in parts of Inverness. Certainly, like the Girt Dog of Ennerdale, the mystery of Satan's visit to Devon gives us food for thought.

5

Wales – and a Miracle

*In one moment I've seen what has hitherto been
Enveloped in absolute mystery,
And without extra charge I will give you at large
A lesson in Natural History.*

Lewis Carroll, *The Hunting of the Snark*

The first hint that anything unusual had occurred was when I returned home from a couple of weeks living on Dartmoor. I had spent a few months studying the area and finally chosen a spot to construct a hide, deep in forestry land overlooking a track that one of the cats had used at fairly regular intervals over the past year. With help from Peter Rolf, the Devon teacher who had seen the cat, I had built the hide using living trees as supports, interwoven with green branches as a screen. Bruised, battered and worn out, I was to have a few days rest, to give any wildlife a chance to investigate and get used to the hide. Then the plan was to spend up to two months keeping watch at night in the hide, hoping at last to photograph the elusive British panther. Everything was organised. Dead bait had been carefully strung up in trees, to try to attract the cat into the area. I had borrowed a small wooden fox-caller – a whistle that sounds like a distressed rabbit. The idea was to set this in the undergrowth a few feet from the hide, and, by the cunning use of a few feet of plastic tube, persuade the cat to investigate the sound and so come within range of my camera. It wasn't as wild a hope as it sounds, because on at least three occasions the cats in the area had approached when men were out lamping for foxes. It was a fairly slim chance; but the only one. Unlike badgers or foxes or other wildlife, the cats appeared to have no set pattern for their night's

137

hunting. It was pointless setting up beside a track they had used the night before, because it might be two months before they passed that way again. They did not seem to feel the need for the security of a familiar path. Even if they followed the same direction each night, they seldom used the same route. But over a year of groundwork made me hopeful of eventual success even if it took another year. And unless a miracle occurred, it could take just that.

And the miracle did occur, in Wales. On my arrival back to civilisation I had been greeted with, 'Have you heard about the ocelot sightings in Wales?' Of course, I hadn't, having been cut off from all news for a few days. I telephoned Ian Tillitson in Tregaron, mid-Wales, to see if he'd heard anything. He hadn't, but promised to check it out. I then settled down with a cup of coffee and turned on the television. It was 'John Craven's Newsround' and behind him flashed up a picture of an ocelot. I was suddenly all attention as I grabbed for my tape recorder. Apparently a man in Wales had photographed and recorded such an animal. I managed to record the cat-like scream as it was played over the air. 'The photographs', said Mr Craven, 'have been sent to be processed and should be back on Thursday'; he moved on to another item, but I was already on the telephone to Broadcasting House in London. Within minutes I was speaking to the 'Newsround' team. No, they had no more information, the item had come from BBC Cardiff. Cardiff were helpful. They hadn't a name or telephone number for the man in the Neath area who took the photographs. However their contact was a Mr Howell Britton. Would I like his number? Would I!

Although excitement was mounting, I still couldn't be sure it was my cats. It could be a hoax, or even a genuine escaped ocelot, but I had a feeling, a conviction, that the breakthrough had finally come. I finally succeeded in contacting Mr Britton. 'Were the animals really confirmed as big ocelots?' was my first question, my fingers tightly crossed. No, he didn't think so, not having looked at pictures of ocelots. Apparently it wasn't done from actual sighting.

'Then who identified them as such?' A local RSPCA inspector had thought they might be so from the description given to him over the phone. 'Are they still around?' was the next question I hardly dared to ask. 'They were last night.' My sigh of relief must have sounded throughout Wales. I asked for a description of the animals.

'A longish body about 5ft in length, a bluish-grey colour with dark stripes and spots. It had upright pointed ears; definitely a cat, about 2ft high. That's of course the adult,' Howell added cheerfully.

'You mean there's young?'

'Two sort of tabby cubs, larger than a domestic cat but much smaller than the adult.'

'What about the photographs?' They wouldn't be back until the weekend. But they should show mother and cubs.

It was three days before I could get to Wales, perhaps the longest three days of my life. A reporter friend, Paul Levine, offered to drive down with me. I had a large cage designed and constructed by a firm near my home and this was dismantled and made ready for transporting. The cost of hiring a van was too high, so we hired a large ladder-rack. Paul would drive my car back, leaving me and the trap in Wales. Howell had arranged for me to stay near the sightings with a Mrs Maggs. At last it was Sunday, the day of departure – a day of pouring rain. I debated whether to call in at Tedburn for my extra camera lenses, but decided against it because of lack of time due to a much later than expected start. It was a decision I was bitterly to regret.

It was dark and still pouring with rain when we reached Neath. Howell and his family welcomed a pair of dripping, tired foreigners with true Welsh warmth. A meal was waiting on the table, even though they had no idea when we would be arriving. Then we were off to Tonmawr to meet Anne Maggs. Within an hour I felt I had known her family all my life and that feeling of warmth has never left me. The next-door neighbours were Steve and Dorothy Joyce. Steve had taken the photographs – and had to tell us of the only disappointment of the day. The cubs had come out perfectly, but mum strangely had not been captured by the camera (see pages 110–12).

But that disappointment didn't matter as I sat in a darkened room watching a bright screen. The clearest slide showed a cub stretched at full length, reaching up to snatch a bag of bait. Its ears were laid back showing a puma-like skull, and the colour was a beautiful silver-grey with dark thin lines and spots along the back. I was reminded of Mrs Christabel Arnold's description of the animal she saw at Crondall, Hampshire: 'It had a white, beige and grey front, and this is the one thing that makes me say it wasn't a puma — it had a beautiful striped red-brown and beigy white-tipped tail. The stripes were as on the back legs with black thin lines.' The Welsh cat was silver-grey instead of reddish-brown, but everything else was the same, the dark thin stripes, the white, beige and grey front, the beautiful banded tail — only the Welsh tail was black-tipped instead of white. And as if that wasn't enough, suddenly from the dark mountain outside came a screaming wail that filled the room. From the forest far across the valley, the cat was announcing its presence. Strangely it never called again during the following two weeks, but that didn't matter, I had at last heard the cry that I had been told of so many times — 'the sound of a hundred cats being murdered!'

Anne Maggs lived alone for three weeks out of four because her husband Dyll and her two younger sons worked in the Shetland Isles. Her eldest son Alan and his wife Jane were staying with her because of the recent events. Anne and Dyll's first sighting of the big cat in November 1981, when they were driving through Tonmawr and a huge grey-striped cat-like animal crossed the road in front of them, has already been mentioned. Including tail, it was about 6ft long, and was very ugly with a bulldog-like muzzle. I remembered the words of Colonel Haines of Brushford, Devon, about the animal he saw: 'It had a brown head, large black prominent eyes and a nose extraordinarily like a pug.'

The next sighting had been by Steve Joyce. Although Anne and Dyll had described the creature to him, he hadn't really taken much notice – not until the day he saw what was apparently the same animal walk across his garden, leap over the fence and vanish up the mountainside behind the house. Then the hunt was on. A few days later a huge grey cat sat on the mountain slope behind the houses and screamed till dawn. Unnerved by the creature, Anne contacted Howell as a local councillor. Not really expecting anything bigger than a European wild cat, nevertheless Howell did his duty and appeared. To his amazement he saw the huge grey cat, plus what appeared to be a pair of cubs, and found Steve and Anne had been stringing bait across Steve's garden in the hope that he could take a photograph. The police were called but they only sighted the cub-like animals which, on their own, were inconclusive. Unfortunately all the activity had scared the animals away from the baiting area, though they were still being seen on the mountainside. Steve managed to take two photographs of cubs taking baits – the photographs I had seen – plus a distant and rather hazy shot of the large animal on the hillside. It was grey with a lighter-coloured front, and sat upright with its head slightly turned away from the camera. Judging by the surrounding vegetation, the cat appeared to be about 2ft high, with extremely long legs and a very small head in comparison with the rest of its body. It had seemed to have a lynx or cheetah shape to it. Less than perfect though the slide was, it was enough to show an animal that, like Alice's Cheshire cat, shouldn't really have been there (see page 109).

Anne's kitchen window overlooks the wild and windy mountain slopes where the animals had been seen. As I was gazing out of the window I noticed the sheep huddling together and milling around on the horizon. Dorothy Joyce came breathlessly to the back door. 'Have you seen the sheep up on the mountain?' she asked. We nodded and the three of us stood watching out of the window. I scanned the hillside and suddenly caught a movement in the other direction. To my excitement an animal suddenly broke cover from the gorse and raced along a sheep track. I shouted as I raced outside, camera in hand. It was without doubt the cub-like animal of the photographs. Then all hell broke loose! From out of the gorse, hard on the heels of the silver-and-black-striped animal, came a second cat, but this time much larger than the first. And it wasn't grey, it was jet black! I was at last seeing the British black panther. Anne's Doberman dog, furiously barking, ran at the fence, and I could see dog and cat at the same time. The cat was about the same size as the dog, but shorter legged. It had a puma-like head with pricked up-right ears, but the body was leopard-like with a sweeping thick, long tail. It moved with a fluid, effortless bounding movement and within seconds it was over the ridge and out of sight. I had run up the slope to the sheep fence, filming as I ran. I leant on the wire, breathless with running and excitement. Few people can ever in their lives be blessed with such a moment. After two years of listening to other people, two years of studying old newspaper files, two years of dreaming, suddenly it had happened. For a few beautiful seconds I had become one of the élite — one of the people who had witnessed the creature that didn't exist; and in daylight, with camera in hand.

I wasn't the only one amazed. Nobody in that Welsh community had suspected they had a black cat, for the only recorded sightings had been of grey animals with stripes. But it confirmed that the animals I was hunting for were indeed in the area, and I was pretty certain that if we searched around we would find witnesses who had seen reddish-brown or tawny big cats. I nervously waited to see if I had captured the black panther on film. The animal had been about 70yd up the mountainside and was a moving target. And, as I hadn't collected my telephoto lens from Tedburn, I had only a standard lens. The only comfort was that I would never have had time to switch lenses, even if it had been with me. It was a nerve racking wait and one I wouldn't wish on my worst enemy. At last the film was processed, and out of all the shots taken, two showed clearly we had it on film at last. It had to be examined through a magnifying glass, so a friend of Jane's, called Bill, kindly sat up all night trying to make an enlargement of the cat. He succeeded, and at last the British panther was on view for all to see, indisputable proof – a beautiful pure black big cat, about the same build as a leopard but with a puma-like head (see page 52).

Malcolm Price, one of Anne and Dyll's friends who was very keen on studying local wildlife, turned up one day to offer his help. He was on holiday, had a few days to spare, and was willing to guide me around the area. Normally I work alone, but I made an exception in Malcolm's case. He excelled in fieldwork, able to sit for hours on a freezing mountain slope without moving a muscle, far better at it than I am. Also, although a few years older than I am he was a lot fitter, and able to cover areas of ground that I found difficult. He even matched me for enthusiasm. The only dispute we had was whether I should be allowed to toddle over the countryside in my usual manner armed only with my camera and my undying faith that the animal was harmless. As well as their marvellous hospitality, the Welsh have another endearing characteristic – their men are very protective towards women; and I don't think they knew quite how to cope with me. Equally, I found it very difficult being protected; I was used to people telling me I was mad, or shrugging their shoulders and washing their hands of me, not to having full-scale arguments on whether I needed looking after. Eventually we compromised, and if Malcolm was able to come with me at night, and wanted to carry a gun, then I agreed. I just didn't mention the odd excursion on my own when he wasn't free.

During the two weeks I worked in Wales, I saw the black cat no more, though I twice spotted the cubs. But through the binoculars Malcolm and Alan one morning saw a strange black cat-like animal on the mountain on the far side of the valley. The surrounding slopes were covered in nearly 2,000 acres of forestry plantation and felling had begun, which was presumably why the cats had moved out into the open. What I did see was a number of sheep carcases in various stages of decomposition, all eaten in the same manner. The head and spine were in position, even if only bones remained; the fleece had been peeled away from the carcase, the lower limbs and jaw were missing and the ribs chewed into. This pattern of killing and eating exactly matched reports that I had of sheep carcases in Sutherland and Ross and Cromarty. I made a complete photographic record of the kills, although a number I think were not actually killed by the cats, but were eaten as carrion; cats are notoriously lazy and sometimes take carrion in preference to making a fresh kill. We also traced a number of sightings, one by forester Bob Pearce, three and a half years before, of a lynx-like animal, and a number of sightings in the area of a reddish-brown big cat. The police at Port Talbot agreed to keep records of any sightings and suspicious sheep kills, and to keep Anne and Malcolm informed.

The next task was to erect my trap on the hillside where the cubs were still being seen. Mr Williams, the farmer, agreed to let me work on his land, and his son, Tudor, promised to keep a watchful eye on the cage. With everyone's help we got the trap in position and baited it with part of a deer carcase provided by Bob Pearce. Malcolm, Anne and the others agreed to check the trap twice a day.

But one last exciting event occurred before I returned home to complete this manuscript. Whilst I was sitting in Steve's house one evening listening to the speakers — for Steve had wired the hillside for sound — the sheep began to get restless and bleat worriedly. Then Anne arrived, pale-faced. Her Doberman had started to rush around barking, and she had opened the front door just in time to see the great shape of a black panther-like cat bounding past the door along the patio. We had noticed pug-like prints before in her garden, beyond the paving. Next morning I cast a perfect paw-print from the mud, and the results were as exciting as the photograph. I already had a number of casts of the cat-prints, but only one, taken by Mr Kingsley Newman from his land at Stoke Gabriel, Devon, was perfect; the others were marred by rain or sand or gravel marks. Mr Kingsley Newman had seen the animal that made his print; it was a large black cat about the size of a leopard. And his print was very interesting. Apart from the fact that it showed the claws very clearly, to the

extent that the animal showed road-wear, it also appeared to
have its pads in a variable size-pattern, like our own hands,
almost like a thumb and fingers ranging down to a little finger. It
was as though the foot was deformed. Casts I had taken at
Tedburn appeared to show the same deformity, but weren't very
clear. Not so the Tonmawr print. Side by side with the Stoke
Gabriel cast, it formed a matching pair. A cat's pads are fairly
evenly sized, but not those of these cats. They were like no cat's
foot I've ever seen: it was like a cross between a hand and a paw. I
studied the blow-up of the cub gripping the bait, and indeed the
paw resembled a hand with fingers. This was the first real
evidence that the cat differed in more than colour from any other
species (see pages 33—4).

When I left Wales my heart was left behind on a windswept
Welsh mountainside. The trap is ready and constantly checked;
Malcolm, Dyll and the others are tracking the surrounding area—
they no longer need me. But I shall go back and continue my
work, for I need just that final piece of the jigsaw, a living animal
to examine. And what better than a young cub – driven out of its
home by the loggers, rejected by its mother because she has
almost certainly mated with the large grey cat and has now left
her juveniles to cope for themselves, whilst she prepares for a
new litter – a cub that already has accepted that humans will
provide food and is used to the scent of having them around?

And if the next few weeks or months produce that final piece of
evidence, what then? My next aim will be to get financial backing
for a research project to enable us to trap an adult animal, fit it
with a tracking collar and then release it back into the wild
where we can study its behaviour in its natural environment, the
British forest. And, of course, to give it a name – this cat that
doesn't exist. For this isn't the end of the story, but only the
beginning.

Appendix
Additional Sightings

Scotland

INVERNESS-SHIRE

Tomich, April 1979. Animal crouched low to the ground. Cat-like, 3–4ft long, tawny with bushy tail. (Resident.)

Inverness, 19 July 1979, about 3.30am. Strange animal huddled in middle of road in housing scheme. Size of a large dog and had a grey and brown striped body with white spot on rear, pointed cat-like ears, back legs like a hare, but no visible tail. When disturbed it spat like a cat and ran away very fast. (Two witnesses.)

Inchrory, 29 October 1979, about 7.30am. Large cat-like animal chasing rabbits in field. Moved with a loping action. About size of Alsatian dog; witness thought must be puma or lioness. (English holidaymaker.)

Cannich, spring 1980. Large dark cat-like creature sitting on roadway. About size of a puma. (Two lady motorists.)

Glen Affric, 30 October 1980. Hillwalkers retracing their route in the snow discovered the tracks of an animal alongside their original footprints. Seemed animal had been following them. Prints cat-like and approximately 4in diameter.

Kiltarlity, 11 December 1980, at 9.00pm. Large brown cat-like animal seen in car headlights. Cleared road in almost one movement. (Motorist.)

Kirkhill, 19 December 1980. Large cat-like creature crossing the road. (Motorist.)

Nairn to Inverness road, Christmas Eve 1981, 1.00am. Just west of junction with access road to MacDermott's site, headlights picked up figure of an animal crossing road. It turned to face the oncoming vehicle and its eyes shone very brightly in the beam. Larger and heavier built than a Labrador dog, tan to light brown in colour and with long thick tail. (Motorist.)

Fort Augustus, 15 May 1981. Puma seen on outskirts of town. (Passing motorist.)

146

Appendix

ROSS AND CROMARTY

Culbokie, 15 November 1979, evening. Large cat-like animal leaping across road. (Schoolboy.)

Muir of Ord to North Kessock road, 19 November 1979, about 10.00pm. Tawny-coloured cat-like animal about 2ft high and 2ft 6in long, with short stocky legs and a smooth coat, seen near Tarradale House.

Findon, 7 December 1979, 8.30am. Large dark-coloured cat-like animal crossed road 2 miles south of Findon, near Tore. (Glasgow man.)

Lochcarron, 17 January 1980, 3.30pm. Large cat-like animal on road. (Motorist.)

Near Dingwall, 26 January 1980, 1.30pm. Large yellow cat-like animal with a long tail. (Two teenage schoolgirls.)

Tore, 7 April 1980. Large paw-marks in sand of a new road. Unfortunately the prints were destroyed by a bulldozer working on the road before they could be photographed. (Police constable.)

A832 Fortrose to Cromarty road, 8 August 1980. Puma-like animal seen at Whitebog. (Hotel manager.)

England

SURREY/HAMPSHIRE/SUSSEX BORDER AREA

Near Crondall, 17 August (year uncertain), 3.30am. Strange cat-like creature in road. Witness unavoidably drove into it with enough force to bend his number-plate yet, apparently unharmed, animal leapt over hedge and disappeared into a field of barley. (Milkman.)

Loxwood, 27 September 1964, about 10.45pm. Very large cat-like animal spotted in headlights. Ambled through roadside hedge and disappeared into darkness. Puma-like. (Driver.)

Witley, 28 September 1964, about 6.15pm. Puma-like animal. (Woman witness.)

Puttenham area, 29 September 1964, 6.45am. Witness came almost face to face with large puma-like animal. (Roadworker.)

Witley, 29 September 1964, 12.30pm. Very large puma-like animal jumped up into tree. Official of the Zoological Society called in to examine claw-marks on trunk found them similar to a puma's. (Schoolmaster.)

Witley, 3 October 1964, about 3.30pm. Very large puma-like animal. (Woman witness.)

Shackleford, 3 October 1964, 4.30pm. Very large puma-like animal on

147

bridle-path. It leapt over an 8ft high hedge to get away. (Two women walkers.)

Elstead, 6 October 1964, 11.00am. Large puma-like animal crossed road in front of bicycle. (Policeman.)

Hascombe, 16 October 1964, 5.00pm. Very large puma-like creature in field near Winkworth Arboretum. (Woman witness.)

Hindhead, 18 October 1964, about 5.00pm. Very large puma-like animal. (Woman exercising her dogs.)

Elstead, 31 October 1964, about 1.30pm. Large puma-like animal ran across field. (Two workmen.)

Ewhurst, 15 December 1964, 4.00pm. Large puma-type animal ran across a field. (Nearby householder.)

Hurtwood, 19 December 1964, about 4.00pm. Large cat-like animal. (Male witness.)

Ewhurst, January 1965. Large cat-like animal. (Two separate witnesses.)

Holmbury St Mary, 15 February 1965, lunchtime. Puma-type big cat crossed garden and walked in direction of cricket ground. (Housewife.)

Dunsfold, 17 May 1965, about 10.40pm. Almost hit an animal in road; resembled a large puma-like cat. (Male driver.)

Dunsfold, 18 June 1965, about 10.00pm. Puma-like animal seen. (Woman exercising dog.) 6 August 1965, 11.45pm. Puma-like animal seen. (Woman witness.)

Cranleigh area, 20 September 1965, about 6.00pm. Puma-like animal seen in copse. (Male witness.)

Chiddingfold, 16 October 1965. Cat drank from a water trough at Hazelbridge Court when witness was attending to her horses; reported to have actually leapt over her head. (Daughter of Viscount Chelmsford.)

Plaistow area, 10 November 1965, 10.15pm. Large puma-like animal crossed road in front of car. (Two male witnesses.)

Godalming area, 11 December 1965, 1.00am. Animal resembling puma crossed road in front of car. (Two male witnesses.)

Worplesdon, 8 April 1966, 7.30pm. Large puma-like animal loping across Whitmore Common. (Woman witness.)

Godalming, 24 April 1966, shortly after midnight. Very large cat-like animal caught in headlights. (Male motorist.)

Dunsfold, 6 June 1966. Puma-like animal seen in copse. (Report received by police.)

Puttenham area, beginning of July 1966. A large number of people saw a puma-like animal.

Puttenham area, 11 July 1966. Puma seen. (Lorry driver.)

Appendix

Ash Green, 14 July 1966, about 9.30am. Large animal seen in grounds of house. Identified by witness as a puma. Ran off across adjoining fields. (Householder.)

Worplesdon area, 14 July 1966, 6.30am. Large puma-like animal visited garden; watched from a distance of only about 25yd. Sprang into a neighbour's garden and out of sight. (Householder.)

Cutt Mill area, 6 August 1966, evening. Puma-like animal reported to police.

Stringers Common, 9 August 1966. Puma-like animal in paddock on farm. (Two male witnesses.)

Pirbright, 15 August 1966, evening. Strange puma-like animal seen. (Male witness.)

Woking area, 16 August 1966, 2.45pm. Puma-like animal seen. (Male witness.)

Grayswood, 22 August 1966, about 9.45pm. Strange animal seen in headlights; puma-like and calmly walking along side of road. Disturbed, it disappeared into the hedgerow. (Motorist.)

Wormley, 30 August 1966, about 3.30pm. Strange animal in field at rear of house. Described as puma-like. Again seen near the house the following day. (Housewife.)

Milford, 4 September 1966. Puma-like animal came out of a tree on Rodborough Common and ran away. (Male witness.)

Thursley, 7 September 1966, 7.30am. Puma-like animal seen. (Woman witness.)

Chiddingfold, 9 September 1966, 7.50am. Puma-like animal in field. It ran away and jumped across a wide stream. (Male witness.)

Hindhead, 18 September 1966, about 2.45am. Puma-like animal crossed road in front of car. (Motorist.)

Worplesdon, 21 September 1966, about 7.10am. Puma-like animal seen by the second tee at Worplesdon Golf Course. (Male witness.)

Hog's Back, 22 September 1966, about 4.00am. Unusual animal seen in headlights on the offside of the road by a five-barred gate. Driver swung car across road so that beams were fully on the creature which crossed the road in leisurely leaps and bounds. Described as a puma.

Stringers Common, 22 September 1966, between 5.00 and 6.00pm. Sighting of puma reported. (Woman witness.)

Hog's Back, beginning of October 1966, early hours of morning. Puma-like animal at side of road. (Motorist.)

Hog's Back, 14 October 1966, early hours of morning. Strange animal on grass verge. Car was stopped and occupants watched it race away across the fields. Described as puma-like. (Two male witnesses.)

Lower Bourne, near Farnham, 28 November 1966, evening. Puma-like animal seen in grounds of house. (Householder.)

Effingham, 8 January 1967, about 11.45am. Puma-like animal seen walking along road. (Male witness.)

Hindhead, 14 January 1967, at 5.00pm. Puma-like animal seen in Punchbowl. (Woman witness.)

Wood Street, 12 May 1967, early evening. Puma-like animal watched in field. One witness was a man who had seen a number of pumas in captivity and he was convinced it was a puma. (Several witnesses.)

Pirbright, 18 July 1967, evening. Puma-like animal sighted in bushes. (Male witness.)

Thursley, 21 July 1967, during morning. From window, large puma-like creature seen strolling through bracken on common land close to house. (Retired Royal Navy captain.)

Chiddingfold, 17 August 1967, about 10.00pm. Very large puma-like animal on grass verge at side of road. (Motor cyclist.)

Bibliography

Bord, Janet and Colin *Alien Animals* Granada (1980)

Brown, Theo *Tales of a Dartmoor Village* Toucan Press (1973)

Clair, Colin *Unnatural History* Abelard-Schuman (1967)

Cobbett, William *Rural Rides* (1830)

Jones, Reverend Edmund of Tranch Newport *A Relation of Apparitions of Spirits in the County of Monmouth and the Principality of Wales* (1813)

MacManus, D. A. *The Middle Kingdom, The Faerie World of Ireland* Colin Smythe (1972)

Ricciuti, Edward, R. *The Wild Cats* Windward (1979)

Rudkin, Ethel H. *The Black Dog* Folklore (1938)

Index

Index